SOLDIER
of LOVE

SOLDIER
of LOVE

An Evolutionary Blueprint
for Thriving in Times of Chaos

TJ BARTEL

FLOWER *of* LIFE PRESS

PRAISE

"*Tj Bartel articulates something of vital importance in his new book* Soldier of Love—*the need for the kind of action that comes from being in true alignment with our deepest self. His vulnerability in sharing some of his most personal struggles paired with the wisdom he has gleaned from a long career of service is potent medicine for these times. His journey from violence and fear to love and peace is riveting. He invites us to make the journey with him so that we, too, may emerge even more committed and certainly better equipped to help bring about healing and face the challenges of this chaotic time. It's well worth the trip!*"

—Rima Bonario, Th.D, Teacher, Speaker, and Author of
*Who Have You Come Here to BE? 101 Possibilities for
Contemplation*

"*Everything that Tj does, he does with his full heart. This book is no different. In* Soldier of Love, *he shows how each one of us can make a positive difference in the world through practical and measurable means. Tj has personally embodied the principles that he teaches, and his genuine desire to instill the same strength and devotion in service to others comes across in his work.*"

—Jaya Prasad, MBA, Columbia University, professional model
and actress

"*As a twenty-year practitioner with the arts and sciences of bodywork, yoga, tantra, qi gong and raw foods, I can attest to the validity of these principles. Tj's wisdom in creating a clear sequence of these truths, coupled with his courageously personal and embodied share, gives way to the fact that we are indeed the vessels for the revolution we have been looking for.*"

—Kylene Baylis

"Soldier of Love *by Tj Bartel is alchemical gold for burned-out spiritual leaders. Bartel's resilience, hard-earned discipline, and devotion to love have woven together and transformed him into the heart-led leader he is today. His 'evolutionary blueprint' gives leaders essential keys to authentically walk their talk by committing to self-care and remaining accountable as they 'warrior up' to do their sacred work and bring about positive change to the world. Having had the privilege to personally receive Tj's teachings and travel with him, I can attest to how aware he is of his needs and those around him. He is a master of his own energy, modeling exactly what he shares in his book.*"

—Lara Wynn, SOUListic Wellness and Ecstatic Living Life Coach, Authentic Tantra® Practitioner and Sexologist, bestselling published author of *Set Sail* and *Sacred Journey: Egypt*

"*As the population reaches a turning point amidst crippling issues and events, Tj Bartel gives us hope. For those desperately seeking meaning, purpose, and solutions to a crisis of confidence, Bartel delivers deep insight, practical experience, and a clear plan through his Blueprints for Life book series with audio and workbook files. If you feel led to release people from their programming, to bring them out of a state of fear, and into a vibration of love and compassion,* Soldier of Love *will help you learn how to use your own unique gifts to inspire, educate, and influence in a new age of enlightenment.*"

—Donna Phelan

"*Tj writes with great clarity and heart about the adversities he has faced in life and how they have shaped his passion for bringing more peace and love to this troubled planet. He clearly outlines the steps we need to take to become our best selves and create more love and peace in our world. His writing is inspirational, and his energy calls us to action. This book is a blueprint for transformation!*"

—Susan Kelly, Consultant

"The author's straightforward, clear prose was viscerally impactful for me. He fearlessly and honestly exposes his own personal journey from an angry, chaotic youth to a man who has achieved a high level of serenity, peace, and love. Truly a 'how-to' book for surviving and rising above the chaos of our current situation and becoming what he calls a 'soldier of love.' He offers a prescription for self-healing and also for healing our world."

—David Allen, Retired Federal Executive

"Soldier of Love *asks us to explore the potential growth that is possible for each one of us. I have always tried to live my life in balance, and this book added so much more to that daily goal for me. I look forward to cultivating the best version of myself through true transformation using Tj's tools. This book offers an open and honest look at living in times of chaos, and supports us to make transformational change in ourselves and in the world around us."*

—Alicia Vasquez

"*The first sentence says it all. 'An inspiring work of art written from the heart by a true energy master and soldier of love.'* In Soldier of Love, *Tj shares his life's journey to convey an important message that the world needs to hear, now more than ever during these times of chaos and uncertainty. Tj's words assure the reader that even when there is war all around us, we can experience love within.* Soldier of Love *gives readers hope by teaching them how to lay down their armor to find the inner strength within, so they can experience a life full of love and joy."*

—Melissa Gentry

"I've known Tj for over forty years and to see his transformation from adolescent to who he is today is simply amazing! Knowing his upbringing, he could have easily gone down a much darker path but through perseverance he found a path of light and love."

—Joel Wyrick, author of *Developing a Wealthy Mindset*

"In Tj Bartel's new book, Soldier of Love, *he explains in detail how to become the best version of yourself. After reading this book you will be inspired to live a vibrant and fulfilling life—making conscious decisions not only on a personal level, but also socially and politically. By telling his own story of choosing love and compassion instead of fear, Tj inspires us to make responsible decisions in life. He underscores how important it is to change inside and outside, bringing vision into action. Intention must be followed by action. He provides many examples of how to do just that."*

—Dr. Helle Trankjær, Chief Physician, Department of Sexology, Roskilde Hospital, Denmark

FLOWER *of* LIFE PRESS

Soldier of Love: An Evolutionary Blueprint for Thriving in Times of Chaos
By Tj Bartel

Book design and cover by Astara Jane Ashley, **www.floweroflifepress.com**

To contact the author, visit **www.TjBartel.com**

Published by Flower of Life Press, *Old Saybrook, CT.*
To contact the publisher, visit **www.floweroflifepress.com**
Download your FREE GIFT: **www.bestsellerpriestess.com/bestseller-priestess**

Library of Congress Control Number: Available upon request.

ISBN-13: 978-1-7349730-4-4

Printed in the United States of America

"Power without love is reckless and abusive and love without power is sentimental and anemic. Power at its best is love implementing the demands of justice, and justice at its best is power correcting everything that stands against LOVE."

—Dr. Martin Luther King, Jr.

DEDICATION

I dedicate this book to my granddaughter Malia Joy Bartel. My dream is that the world Malia raises her children in is rooted in love, compassion, tolerance, and equality. I am committed to doing everything in my power to make sure that by the time she joins the workforce, equal pay for women in our country will be fully and completely realized.

Because fear and love cannot coexist, this book addresses the danger of fear-based politics and belief systems in hopes that drastic changes will be made before Malia is old enough to vote. It is my intention that this contribution sheds light on the areas that have been hidden away in the darkness for eons so that they can be addressed and healed. May this book empower people to be better and do better for themselves, each other, and for future generations.

CONTENTS

ACKNOWLEDGMENTS

My acknowledgments must start with my son Dereck Myles Bartel. Unexplainably wise beyond his years from the time he was just a little boy, Myles has been a clear and articulate voice of reason for me. His intellect and ability to speak his truth has amazed me over and over again. His words and opinions first opened my eyes to the dysfunction of our educational and religious leaders and the lack of understanding of what children really need to be learning in school. I never attempted to curb his rebellious questioning because I wanted to raise him as an independent thinker and an authentic individual. (And also because he was almost always right.) I was in college when Myles was born, and really still a kid myself. As his father, I sought to keep his best interest at the forefront of my consciousness, which kept me from getting into too much trouble as a young man. In many ways, we raised each other. I am proud of who we both turned out to be, and I am insanely grateful for my incredible son. Who knows where I would be without the gift of Myles, and I am deeply thankful for every single moment that we have together.

I want to acknowledge and thank Dr. Rima Bonario from the bottom of my heart. She has been a guiding light and a pillar of strength for me to become a bestselling author and a better man. Her consistent support and wisdom have been an endless source of fuel for me in finding the best ways possible to fulfill my sacred contract and bring my mission to fruition. Rima's unconditional love, passion, and brilliance have inspired me to keep showing up strong, no matter how many challenging obstacles appear. Rima is a profound presence in this world. I am forever thankful for her contribution to this book, my mission, and my life. I would not be who I am today if it wasn't for her.

I want to acknowledge Joel Wyrick for being a loyal and trusted friend and adviser for over forty years. He is a shining example of a powerful and successful man with true integrity. I am grateful for the dozens of incredibly memorable vacations, intellectually stimulating conversations, and massive amounts of laughter that we have shared throughout our adult lives.

I want to acknowledge my good friend, colleague, and teacher, Charles Muir, for always being there for me when I needed him. He is a powerful force for good on this planet. Through his many battles, including beating cancer, Charles continues to be a source of unconditional love for the countless people he has blessed with his work. I am grateful for the many great times that we have shared and for the profound lessons that I have learned from being his friend, colleague, and student.

I want to extend my appreciation for Astara Jane Ashley and the Flower of Life Press team for the love, support, and expertise they have shown in making the dream of this book into a reality in such a short time, especially during these challenging and chaotic times. While in the midst of a hurricane and without power, Astara charged her cell phone in her automobile in order to stay connected and keep the momentum going. She is a model of dedication and devotion.

I want to thank the many other beloved friends and colleagues who have inspired, supported, and influenced me on my road to success with this book and in life. I am grateful to all who took the time to read early drafts of *Soldier of Love* and shared their praise and insights.

And I am grateful to you, dear reader, for purchasing this book and supporting my mission to make this world a better place for future generations.

INTRODUCTION

"I've lost the use of my heart / But I am still alive / Still looking for the light."

"Soldier of Love" by Sade

"Lay down your arms ... and love me peacefully."

"Soldier of Love" by The Beatles

I was eight years old when I reached a fork in the road of my life, facing a life-defining decision. Had I made a different choice, I would have had a very different experience—a life in "the system," one of habitual incarceration. I was lucky; grace intervened, and love won out. It took years for the fullness of that shift to manifest. My life's work now centers on love: the love between partners, love for the planet, and love as an act of service. Out of the chaos and violence of my early years, I have become a devotee of love and peace.

I was born in September 1963, just a month and a half after the Beatles recorded the song "Soldier of Love" for the first time. Two months after my birth, John F. Kennedy was assassinated. These two events are like the bookends surrounding my birth, forming two banks that the river of my life had flowed between—*love* and *peace* on one side and *fear* and *violence* on the other.

At the start of the 1960s, civil rights for black Americans had pushed to the forefront of political discussion. Segregation and the Jim Crow laws of the South were being challenged. The sexual revolution was also gaining momentum, and women were finding and using their voices. People wanted something other than what they were being offered by the powers that be. There was plenty of love and peace and plenty of fear and violence.

Things intensified as the decade progressed. In 1964, President Lyndon Johnson sent the first American troops to Vietnam. Anti-war protests became a regular part of the American zeitgeist. Around the age of four, I remember seeing murals appear all over the commercial buildings in my neighborhood. Flowers, peace signs, hearts, and the word *love* popped up everywhere. I was drawn to them. Every boulevard stop sign had the word *war* spray-painted beneath the word *stop*. People were rebelling against authority, rebelling against the confining structures and rise of the commercialism of the 1950s, against the war machine and political agenda. They grew their hair and wore fringe, beads, and bell-bottoms. There was an acknowledgment of the systemic oppression that held down anyone who didn't fit neatly inside of pre-defined packages. There was a general sense that our government was being run by warmongers who cared more about their twisted agendas and their personal power-plays than life itself; it was an (r)evolutionary time in American history.

I can't help but see the parallels between then and now, only the war we are losing is the war on poverty, racism, and civility. We are also losing the battle against climate change, the gender gap, and now the global pandemic. Civil unrest is growing, and once again, the youth, the disenfranchised, and the struggling working class are demanding something better. As harsh as this time feels, it is paving the way for our nation and our world's evolution.

As a nation, we are at a crossroads, and we will have to decide. In our fight to bring about a better world, will we succumb to the fear and violence of those we seek to depose, using the same violent means to bring about change? Or will we carve out a different path forward? There is a natural tension that often arises between whether the "right" place to work at this is in the personal arena or the political and social arenas. This is a false fight that could cause us to lose big if we stay stuck in it. We have *both* inner and outer, personal, and collective battles to face. Let's each mine our individual story and the story of our nation's history to find the wounds that must be healed and energetically alchemized from lead to gold. My hope is that we are up for the inner and outer alchemy required at this crossroads. My desire is that we are older and wiser now, and as we "warrior up," we will seek to be evolutionary warriors—soldiers of love who do the inner work to change so that the collective can heal.

Within these pages, you will find stories and lessons that will guide you on a journey towards being the best possible version of yourself. Then you will learn how to help others take the same steps on their journey to awakening their inner Soldier of Love. Once you have read this book in its entirety, you will have a clear-cut and easy-to-follow path to bettering yourself and the world while being rewarded with abundance in all areas of your life. Enjoy the ride...

"Every day the average person fights epic battles never told just to survive."

—Ken Poirot

"You don't run from the people who need you. You fight for them. You fight beside them. No matter the cost. No matter the risk."

—Rick Yancey

Chapter 1

THE MAKING OF
A SOLDIER OF LOVE

Much like life in 2020, my childhood was filled with uncertainty, chaos, and violence while, at the same time, rich with love, adventure, and excitement. Born into a family with five older sisters, the family topped out with seven girls and two boys, myself included. My brother was born when I was in high school, so I grew up as an only boy in the 1960s and '70s when free love and sexual exploration were the norms. For me, there was always a dichotomy or even a sense of duality expressed in my everyday life. I was plagued with poverty, violence, and fear—but there was also a lot of love, laughter, and dancing. I believe that the story of my climb out of the violence of my youth, propelled by the love that I found there, can shine a light on a possible path forward out of the fear and anger that plague our world today.

A Rough Ride

I was terrified of my father and was bullied a lot in school. We were continually relocating, almost always in low-income and minority neighborhoods where blonde hair and blue eyes were like having a target on my back. When I was in fourth grade, my family moved to a home on King Road in east side San Jose, California. I went to Miller Elementary School, where I quickly became the focus of a

Mexican gang led by a kid in my class named Raul and his two pals Tino and Manuel. Altogether they were twenty or thirty kids.

These kids knew where I lived and how I walked to school. Every day they waited to beat me up. Most days, I would run from them, but now and then, I would get tired of running and fight back. I would lose badly because I was so outnumbered. Eventually, I learned to leave extra early and to jump fences rather than walking down the streets where they waited. I spent my recesses and lunchtimes sitting in front of the principal's office so that I could quickly step inside for safety.

I had figured out how to get to and from school and spend my breaks in peace, but it didn't last. One day a kid I had never met before walked up to where I was sitting in front of the office and sucker-punched me. I was able to wrestle him to the ground and rough him up with little effort. This went on for weeks until I asked him why he kept coming back even though he knew that he was just going to lose every time. He shared that Raul and his gang told him that if he didn't come after me, they would hurt his little sister—a second-grader. After that, we became friends. We ate lunch together often, and his sister was never bothered.

As if my school wasn't stressful enough, my home life was also quite scary at times. I was terrified of my abusive father; when he was home, I stayed outside whenever possible. I had figured out how to stay safe at home and in school. Plus, I had a new friend. Life was looking up.

Things were going fine until one day when I had to use the bathroom and didn't wait to be sure the coast was clear. I snuck into the restroom, hoping for the best, but one of Raul's gang members saw me go in. He whistled, and, in what seemed like seconds, more than a dozen gang members rushed into the bathroom. I didn't even have a chance to go. Then in came Raul. He said, "You have three choices, *güero*. We can flush your face down the toilet, beat the shit out of you like old times, or you can pull down your pants and show us your little white dick." I was simply too dumbfounded to answer. I figured that they would want to push my face into the toilet, and I would not let them.

Raul continued, "I'm going to count to three and then choose for you." When he said three, I began swinging. I got a few punches in before they wrestled me to the floor and held me down while Raul pulled my pants and underwear down to my knees. They all laughed hysterically then left me lying on the damp and filthy floor. I had never felt more humiliated in my life. I left school that day, burning with humiliation and anger. But home was no escape.

That night, my father arrived home from work to find my mother's first husband, Tom, in the house and holding my younger sister Tracy on his lap. My father heard Tracy calling Tom, "Daddy." This was obviously a sore spot. When Tom left, my father let his rage fly. It began with verbal abuse that escalated into physical abuse. He beat my mother half to death. It seemed to go on for hours. I tried to intervene, but my sisters held me back for my own protection. I screamed and fought but was unable to help my mother. I remember yelling, "I'm going to kill you!" over and over again. I watched in terror while my father punched my mother repeatedly in the face while calling her all kinds of horrible names. He dragged her by her hair across the kitchen floor and shoved her face into the open garbage container filled with jagged cans that cut into her beautiful face. He finally took her into their room and shut the door. But it was far from over for me.

I waited until everyone was asleep and silently crept into the kitchen to get the largest butcher's knife we had. I crept as quietly as I could into my parents' bedroom. My mother was lying face down completely covered up, and my father was face up snoring with his mouth wide open. I stood over him and clasped the knife with both hands. I raised the knife up and focused intently on the center of his throat. I was calm and focused as I pictured exactly where the blade would enter his neck—taking his life. The urge to kill was greater than anything I had ever experienced. I felt righteous, strong, and fearless.

But after visualizing the act being completed, my future flashed before my eyes. I was taken away from my family and put into a juvenile detention center where I wound up killing someone else. After several years I was put in a series of horrid foster homes and went in and out of juvie. Then I saw myself as a 40-year-old man. My head was clean-shaven, my face was scarred, and my muscled body was covered with ugly tattoos. In my vision, I *knew* that I had spent most of my adult life in prison and had taken several more lives. At that moment, I saw the path that lay before me, accepted it as my new destiny, and felt completely comfortable with it.

However, just as I was about to run my father through, my mother moved slightly. In that split second, I realized that my mother would wake up to see me murdering her husband and be more traumatized by that than from the beating itself. I felt like I was being advised by my potential future self to sacrifice my plan for my mother's sake. My future-self was right. My mother would lose both of us and spend the rest of her life blaming herself! I loved my mother, and I couldn't do that to her. After this powerful, albeit disappointing realization, I returned to the kitchen, put the knife back in the drawer, and went back to bed. Unable to sleep, I just stared at the ceiling until morning.

That day I took my usual route to school, avoiding the gang and getting there even earlier than usual. I was typically the first one there when the teacher opened the door, but on this day, she was late. More students arrived until the whole class was there waiting. Eventually, Raul started telling everyone about what they had done to me the day before in the bathroom. He taunted me repeatedly, saying, "Tell them what we saw, *güero*." He kept on until I snapped.

I grabbed him by the hair and began slamming his head into the concrete wall. His blood was pouring down my arms, splattering across the wall, and splashing my face. His body went limp, and his friends were punching and kicking me, but I was unphased. Out of nowhere, a big white kid I had never seen before grabbed me and swept me away. I did not return to school until the next morning. I had put a small steak knife in my sock, and I walked to school without fear that day. When I arrived, Raul was not in class, and his gang avoided me like the plague.

It was a short-lived victory. When I got home that night, I was put on the back of a commercial flatbed truck that took me from San Jose to Oxnard, outside Los Angeles, to stay with my mother's brother. Uncle Albert took me straight into his garage, where he cut my "hippy" hair, giving me my first flat top. While I finished out the school year in Oxnard, my mother spent weeks in the hospital, and my father spent some time in jail.

Summer vacation rolled around, and I stayed at my uncle's. I learned to do jumping jacks and pushups and channeled my energy in healthier ways. I was there the whole summer without getting into a single fight. It was the most normal summer I had ever experienced. It was a break in my life's trajectory that would save me from the darkest version of myself. I pray for that same kind of intervention for our nation.

The Promise, the Lie, and the Truth about America

"We hold these truths to be self-evident, that all men are created equal, that they are endowed by their Creator with certain unalienable Rights, that among these are Life, Liberty and the pursuit of Happiness. That to secure these rights, Governments are instituted among Men, deriving their just powers from the consent of the governed, That whenever any Form of

*Government becomes destructive of these ends, it is the Right of
the People to alter or to abolish it, and to institute new government, laying its foundation on such principles and organizing its
powers in such form, as to them shall seem most likely to effect
their Safety and Happiness."*

—Preamble, U.S. Declaration of Independence

America's Declaration of Independence was a paradigm-shattering
document, something we can all be very proud of as Americans. It
was indeed a profoundly revolutionary idea that all men are created equal. But the promise of this document has yet to be realized.
There is simply no denying it. The promise that America would be
a place where all people would have Freedom, Equality, Protection, Justice, and Liberty has not been kept. In fact, it has been broken over and over again. We, the people, must demand that these
promises be kept. We want what was promised to us, and we must
continue to demand equality for all.

History is replete with leaders who took on this challenge, bringing us ever closer to the perfect Union dreamed of at the country's founding. America's 16th president, Abraham Lincoln, was
a courageous, visionary leader and statesman who saw the nation
through its most important moral and political crises to date. President Lincoln saw the need and stepped up by issuing the Emanci-
pation Proclamation on January 1, 1863, making slavery illegal. But
rather than complying and being lawful and patriotic, the South
betrayed our president and our government and committed an act
of treason in starting a civil war.

Unwilling to make do with fewer profits, or make any social adjustments to their privileged way of life born off the backs of
slave labor, southern slave owners and political leaders clung to
the stories they told themselves about their victimization at the
hands of an overreaching federal government. These stories and
long-held beliefs of racial superiority formed a kind of virus of

the mind, a type of twisted and backward conditioning that had them believing that freeing slaves was a violation of *their* rights. It was a deadly delusion.

According to the 1889 study of the war performed by William F. Fox and Thomas Leonard Livermore, approximately 620,000 soldiers died from combat, accident, starvation, and disease during the Civil War. But the horror of death did not stop there.

On the evening of April 14, 1865, Abraham Lincoln, a Republican, was assassinated by a confederate sympathizer and famous actor named John Wilkes Booth. He was murdered just five days after the traitor general Robert E. Lee finally surrendered, rendering president Lincoln and the Union the victor. Despite this huge victory, many confederate sympathizers refused to free their slaves. Eventually, freedom was granted, but then a whole host of systemic policies such as Black Codes and Jim Crow laws popular in the South made sure that freed slaves were stymied at every turn as they tried to forge a life for themselves and their families.

While we have made some progress over the years, the belief that whites are somehow a superior race persists even today. Unbelievably, those loyal to the confederacy's views have now taken over the party of Lincoln. It's not new; it has been happening slowly for decades.

I was five years old the night of April 4, 1968, when Dr. Martin Luther King Jr. was assassinated for pleading with the American government to honor the promises of equal treatment for all. Once Dr. King began leading peaceful protests, he was deemed a threat by his oppressors. His home was bombed twice, and he was attacked, beaten, and arrested many times before he was eventually assassinated. All he asked for was what was promised to all Americans. He led powerful peaceful protests against inequality and segregation. Still, the racist good-old-boy system simply could not bear the thought of him raising awareness and succeeding in his cause. So they killed him.

Not My American Dream

"Unresolved grief inside a person is tragic; unresolved grief inside a nation is catastrophic: It releases enormous aggression."

—Valier Kaur, *See No Stranger, A Memoir* and *Manifesto of Revolutionary Love*

I grew up thinking that America was always the "good guy," the virtuous and fearless leader of the free world, and, therefore, the greatest nation on Earth in just about every way. Our most beloved television shows and movies depicted the American people as honest and hard-working, with true integrity and hearts of gold. The story we told ourselves was that our government was all about furthering the values of truth, personal freedom, and liberation from tyranny. Watching nightly newscasts, I grew up believing that every war happened because we were defending liberty and standing up for those who could not stand up for themselves.

It was a common theme: Democracy would save the people from tyrannical rulers across the globe—and we would lead the way. I knew this to be true until I had enough real information to experience a very rude awakening. My experience of awakening from this illusion is reminiscent of the story of Ron Kovic, played by Tom Cruise in the movie *Born on the Fourth of July*. Like Ron, I thought that the most courageous and patriotic thing that I could do was join the U.S. military and dedicate my life to fighting for my country. Like Ron, my perspective changed drastically.

I very much wanted to join in the fight in Vietnam like my uncles, cousins, and brothers-in-law. I planned to join after high school and get my college education paid for by being a special forces phenom like several of my cousins. These guys were my heroes. They were big, strong, masculine role models who were incredible fighters and excellent soldiers. Two of these cousins were identical twins, Russel and Recil. They were the true definition of badasses, both Special Forces—one a green beret and the other an Airborne Ranger. They were each six foot two and 225 pounds of pure muscle forged through martial arts, boxing, and street-fighting. Their father, Uncle Jack, was my father's big brother who fought in the Korean war. I wanted to be a badass like them and figured that I would also fight in a war one day.

However, one day, my cousin Russel sat me down and explained that it was not what I thought. He said, "Tj, you don't want to sacrifice your life for these people because the truth is that we are not always the good guys."

Shortly after that, my brother-in-law Rick admitted to me that what he did all those years while he was in Vietnam was horrific. He flew into heroin factories, killed everyone, and took all of the heroin. He said that he had to kill women and children in self-defense. He described in detail how he would crush their skulls with his boots as they tried to stab him or blow up his chopper with grenades and makeshift bombs.

John F. Kennedy was another great visionary leader, perhaps one of the last we've had, who stood up to those who believed they were racially superior. He made civil rights a priority, and he, too, was assassinated. Since then, we have been mired in wars, cold and hot, and lived with the threat of nuclear proliferation.

America is no longer a leader in the world. We are not showing the way forward. Those sacred principles that gave rise to our precious democracy are now in danger. And when people speak out and attempt to shed light on injustice, they sometimes get arrested, terrorized, or murdered. Don't get me wrong I love my country! I love what we stand for—truth, liberty, and the pursuit of happiness—just not when the reality doesn't match those ideals.

The Soldier's Dilemma

Like many in my community, I was deeply disappointed with the 2016 election results. Since then, we have been witnessing what appears to be a lack of empathy for people in need of health care and equitable economic policies, constant amplification and exploitation of political divisions, the inability to denounce racism, the active display of sexism, and a bungled response to CoVid-19.

Rather than encouraging people to make short-term sacrifices for the good of all, our president made light of the pandemic and the importance of wearing masks and social distancing. He promoted questionable treatments. Against the recommendations of the scientific community, he encouraged the premature re-opening of the nation. The administration's response to the different protests we have seen in 2020 has been to embrace those who demanded access to haircuts and bars but criticize and even harass those protesting civil rights violations. A measured and heartfelt response to both the CoVid-19 crisis and the murder of George Floyd could have served to unify and calm a deeply divided and fearful country. Instead, that opportunity was squandered, and the response has made things worse.

I felt the urge to respond to all of this dysfunction in kind. My initial writing on this topic had to be edited many times. Eventually, I came to see it as a test of my own commitment to be a Soldier of

Love. Conversations with friends and colleagues had me looking deeply at this, facing the work to discern whether my words were seeking to express both truth and love, rather than just adding gasoline to the already burning fire in our nation. Were we already at war? Or was I starting the war? Would my voice inspire and fight for the underdog, or lead me back into the darkest parts of myself? At times, this can feel like a mighty fine line and one that I often struggle with. I am human, after all.

Fighting From Love

"Unconditional Love really exists in each of us. It is part of our deep inner being. It is not so much an active emotion as a state of being. It's not 'I love you' for this or that reason, not 'I love you if you love me.' It's love for no reason, love without an object."

—Ram Dass, (May 6, 1931 - December 22, 2019)

One of the most powerful teachings I received around this issue came from a visit I had with master teacher Ram Dass. I was teaching a workshop on Maui, and we had the chance to sit and "talk story" with him as he shared stories about the people whose pictures were displayed on his altar. There were saints, sages, gurus, and historical figures who represented love and spiritual enlightenment. The very last one was a cartoon caricature of Donald Trump. The illustration was surrounded by thousands of tiny little words that were too small for me to read.

When I asked Ram Dass why he had this image of Donald Trump on this altar next to people who had devoted their lives to peace, love, and spiritual enlightenment, he chuckled. Then the caricature was handed to me. I tried to read the tiny little words around the edges and asked what the words signified. Ram Dass replied, "These words are what I say to him, and what I will continue saying to him every single day for the rest of my life: I do not know you from your soul, I only know you from your karma. But how could anyone not have compassion for a soul that has such karma?"

I instantly felt a profound shift in my body. Before that, when I would watch Donald Trump on the television insulting people and behaving in ways that I considered cruel and irresponsible, I would feel anger and adrenaline would pump through my veins. I would have the desire to punch him in his face so hard his hair would fall off. But at that moment, I suddenly and deeply felt only compassion for him. This was a great relief to my nervous system. I understood at that moment that my belief that human beings do the best they can with the resources that they have applied to Donald Trump as well. I was able to hold on to that compassion for a long time. And then came 2020, and it fell away.

The Mirror in My Dreams

While writing this manuscript and seeking to integrate both sides of myself, I had a strange dream. I was sitting around a large bonfire with about twenty of my closest friends. There were also about a dozen or so strangers seated by the fire. Out of the blue, Donald Trump walked past me. He was naked, holding his clothes and shoes in his arms. He was nervous and uncomfortable looking for a safe place to get dressed. A few guys I didn't know got up and aggressively approached him with violent intentions. I stood up and placed myself between Trump and these guys, saying, "Nobody touches him."

One of the guys started to puff himself up to challenge me. I said, "Look, I don't like his behavior or policies, but nobody lays a finger on him unless they want to go through me to do it." The guys measured me for a moment, could see I was serious, and then sat back down. Trump continued walking past unharmed. He returned later fully dressed, looking like he did in his forties. He gave me a wink, and I said, "Looking good, Don." He smiled gratefully and walked off in peace. I woke up feeling compassion and forgiveness for Donald Trump.

I recognize that it can seem like we are giving a pass to egregious behavior when we act from compassion in the face of abuse. But just as I saw killing my father would deliberately add more trauma to my family and destroy me, we too have to find ways to right the wrongs and make better, more loving, choices while not surrendering our own capacity for love. We have to lean into what Dr. King called "the fierce urgency of now" to demand systemic and individual change, while still conducting ourselves with dignity and grace, seeking change by peaceful, non-violent means. This includes monitoring the violence in our words and in our hearts. It is far from an easy task. Yet it is well worth the struggle to achieve it alongside the effort to create a more fair and just America.

It is this struggle that is at the very foundation of this book and my life. The inner war mirrors the outer war. This is the war that the Soldier of Love is called to fight. Yes, it is easier now to revert to the parts of myself that are angry and indignant. At times it feels like anger is the seat of my power. However, the real power comes from deep and abiding love. My work is to continue embodying the truth that it is possible to love someone and, at the same time, condemn their behavior. We love because that is who we are. We seek healing and change because of that love.

It's Darkest Before the Dawn

The failures of the last four years must be named before they can be healed. The Trump administration has been actively working to roll back protections for minorities, immigrants, clean water, clean air, protected land, and endangered species. We had come a long way as a nation in many areas, but not nearly far enough. And now it seems we are going backward. Consider these facts about our great country:

Continued Gender Inequality

In 1923, the National Woman's political party introduced the Equal Rights Amendment (ERA) to Congress intending to provide for the legal equality of the sexes and prohibit discrimination on the basis of sex. It took nearly fifty years for Congress to pass the amendment. Since 1972, the ERA has been waiting for enough states to ratify it in order to become part of the constitutional guarantees to more than 50 percent of the American population.

Continued Poor Health-Care

The United States has the lowest life expectancy and highest suicide rates among the top eleven countries in the world. The first-ever attempt to provide health-care to all Americans has been gutted and is in danger of being repealed completely—in the midst of a dangerous pandemic. At the time of this writing, more than almost 5.7 million cases of the CoVid-19 have been recorded in the United States alone. More than 177,000 Americans have lost their lives, and over 30 million have lost their jobs. Due to mass closures, 1.5 billion children are out of school, homelessness is worse than ever, and civil unrest has become the norm.

The Growing Political Divide, Election Irregularities, Low Voter Confidence

The divisive political rhetoric is infused with overt racism, and hate crimes are on the rise. Election meddling and Cyber warfare by foreign governments, voter suppression, and voter intimidation are happening right out in the open. It's no wonder people feel our democracy is being threatened by corruption at the highest levels of government, including the presidency.

The Climate Crisis

In the midst of all the chaos, it may be easy to forget that our planet is still in peril. The Earth is being harmed by human behavior to the degree that may very well lead to an uninhabitable planet. The science has been clear for decades. The temperature of the atmosphere is rising to dangerous levels, causing more frequent natural disasters. Furthermore, our species has been harming the planet in many more ways than just climate change. Oil spills caused by offshore rigs, damaged tankers, or pipelines cause devastating damage to the oceans, beaches, and all their inhabitants. These spills can create an oil slick that spreads across hundreds of nautical miles and can last many decades. The continuing crises of air pollution, fracking, and dying coral reefs all reflect our betrayal of Mother Nature.

A Brighter Day Is Coming

Whether it's issues of race, free and fair elections, gender equality, public health, or the climate crisis, *we the people* are in need of guidance and support more than ever. There is no doubt that we have reached a boiling point, fed up with the outdated systems that have created this bleak state within the United States and the world as a whole. It's hard not to feel angry or hopeless in the face of such incompetence and corruption.

There is a true leadership void. What seems to be emerging is that the kind of change that needs to happen cannot come from a small number of elected leaders but only from a massive shift in consciousness and the energy brought on by people uniting and rising up to take a stance for something better.

We seem to be living in a leaderless period in history. Perhaps, this is because *we* need to be the leaders we are looking for. It is people like us who will ignite the flames of change that will burn through the resistance and break the chains of bigotry, inequality, corruption, and oppression.

> *Now is the time of the Evolutionary Warrior.*
> *The Everyman (or Everywoman!) Leader.*
> *The Soldier of Love.*

Millions of us are sensing the serious need and urgency to address it as we wake up to join this crucial movement. We are emerging from the dark depths of what feels like mass hypnosis. As we wake up, we are finding each other, organizing ourselves, and preparing and training for what's next.

Now is the time to become the highest functioning versions of ourselves while creating the highest functioning and most powerful, efficient, and productive collective ever assembled. *We, the people,* are the best, and perhaps only, hope for our democracy to survive. Just like my younger self, we need a break in our collective trajectory—a reset to save us from the darkest version of ourselves.

Tj 2.0

I grew up surrounded by women inside my home and surrounded by minorities outside. I also had the rare experience of being a white male without other white males to bond with. It wasn't until I moved to Saratoga so I could attend Westmont High School that I realized that, as a white person, I was not a minority. This sensitized me to issues of race in a unique way as I have always felt at home with people of color, even though it wasn't always safe or fun for me. I moved from one tough neighborhood to another until attending Westmont, which was a predominantly white high school. I could literally count all of the black people at the school on one hand. It was surreal. I didn't fit in any better, though, because my mannerisms, gait, and speech patterns weren't the norm for a white kid with blond hair and blue eyes. I had grown up in the hood, and it showed. My saving grace was being a good athlete. I played basketball and excelled in track, setting many records for the high jump, some of which still stand today.

Another deeply defining trait from my younger years was my hatred for bullies. Combating them gave me a place to channel my aggression and skills as a fighter—one guided by love for others. When I witnessed other kids getting bullied, I felt compelled to take on the bullies, putting them in their place. I wanted to protect the underdogs in every fight. Honestly, I came by my passion for defending those who are in danger or oppressed through my own lived experience. Fighting against racism and bullies is a part of who I am at the deepest level; it's a true gift from the harsh experiences of my early life.

At just ten years of age, I unintentionally read my first self-help book, *The Tao of Jeet Kwon Do* by Bruce Lee. It captured my imagination. After that, I became fascinated with human potential, personal growth, and self-mastery. It was a way out of the chaos of my life. In my early twenties, I became part of an elite martial arts fighting team. This focused my aggression and penchant for fighting in even more positive ways. Along with my martial arts team, I began to study a variety of self-mastery techniques, including those taught by Tony Robbins.

My interest in human behavior and personal growth inspired me to pursue a bachelor's degree in Psychology. After attending the Tony Robbins Mastery University, I discovered a real talent for transforming lives positively. My years of growing up in a household with seven sisters had given me an edge with women, and my friends were constantly asking me to coach them so that they could be more successful with the ladies. There was no trick. I just genuinely loved, respected, and trusted women. They were the safe ones in my life.

At one of Tony's signature programs, Date with Destiny, I uncovered my life's mission: to spread massive amounts of love and joy to as many people as humanly possible, while being massively rewarded. My transformation into a Soldier of Love was complete. But I wasn't exactly sure how I would turn that passion into a vocation.

I knew that supporting people in having satisfying and loving relationships was a big part of that calling. I eventually found Tantra, or sacred sexuality work, which brought together my passion for personal transformation through intimacy and relationships. I dove in head-first and became the foremost expert on hands-on sexual awakening using, among other things, sacred spot massage. I have helped thousands of individuals and hundreds of couples find great joy and fulfillment, as well as spiritual evolution, through sacred sexuality.

In more than twenty years since then, I have dedicated myself to excellence in the personal development field, mastering the skills required to succeed as a coach, author, and educator. I have developed potent and innovative personal growth techniques that integrate perennial wisdom from the Taoist, Vedic, and Tantric traditions, Egyptian mystery school teachings, modern neuroscience, and guided meditation. My goal is to create lasting and meaningful change and transformation in individuals and the world. One of my greatest joys is supporting people in creating exquisite relationships that will ultimately lead to positive benefits for themselves and everyone in their lives—something I dive into deeply in my book *The Great Lover Blueprint for Men* and the soon-to-be-released *Blissful Couple Blueprint*, both part of my Blueprints for Life series.

Today, my focus is on teaching online and in-person workshops—especially teaching others with a passion for making the world a better place—and how to do so while becoming financially successful. It is exciting to help a wider audience find the answers they need to be the very best version of themselves and create a more loving and conscious world.

This has taken on a true sense of urgency for me as it's clear that, just like my eight-year-old self, America is at a crossroads and in a fight for its life. We, the people, need to make a choice, and each of us who feels the call of the Soldier of Love has a pivotal role to play.

The American Dream 2.0

The United States is among the wealthiest nations in the world, yet it is far from healthy mentally, physically, or emotionally. So many people are not able to develop themselves into their full potential. They need help, and our leaders are failing them and us. Here's where you come in.

Imagine that saving the world was a professional or Olympic sport. The call has gone out to find those who are so dedicated to this change, those who are willing to make it their life's mission to become the greatest, most successful, and best-trained change agents on the planet. This elite team's roster has just been announced, and we are all on it. I am up for the challenge and, since you are reading this book, I know you are too. Now it's time to hit the ground running.

Imagine a world based on the principles of love, safety, and connection rather than fear, scarcity, and competition. Imagine people united by core beliefs that prioritize making the ever-elusive American Dream an actual reality.

Imagine a government that unequivocally defends the constitution and amendments as well as the protection and liberation for all of the people. A government that is *truly* for the people, by the people. One that helps to create a global system that supports equal treatment for all of the people, all of the time, regardless of gender, sexual orientation, or ethnicity. A world where hate groups are no longer tolerated, and all people live together in harmony.

Imagine a system where everyone gets to vote without massive roadblocks and voter suppression tactics getting in the way.

These imaginings give me great joy and a real sense of purpose. I have faced criticism for articulating this fantasy. But, is it truly so unrealistic to believe that peace, harmony, freedom, and equality can be achieved?

Let's start small. Here's the truth: Millions of people have transformed their lives by reading books and taking online courses. A good portion of the population loves to learn and actively seeks to better themselves. Beyond that, there are countless things that were once believed to be utterly impossible and are now everyday experiences. For example, imagine we could jump in the Delorean, like Michael J. Fox in *Back to the Future*, and travel back in time to America just fifty years ago to try to convince people that they will soon be able to do all of their shopping without ever leaving the house. Imagine their surprise when they learn that just by pushing some buttons—that aren't even really buttons!—on a small pocket device, everything their heart desires would be brought to their front door within a couple of days. Such an experience would be hard to fathom.

Now imagine what it must have been like when people first discovered how to build a fire. That must have been an awesome scene seeing these faces of ancient "scientists" when they figured out how to create friction and harness the element of fire itself. Automobiles, electricity, the light bulb, telephones, airplanes, spacecraft, people on the moon, computers, laptops, cell phones, and the internet are all examples of the impossible becoming possible.

You might be thinking, "Yes, but those are *things,* not government policies." Consider for a moment how revolutionary the concept of a country with no king was. America was once just a dream, and it evolved into a superpower. Evolution itself is the real superpower. And life on Earth has some experience with that.

New studies have suggested that some 4.47 billion years ago—just 60 million years after the Earth took its shape and 40 million years after the moon was formed—an object about the size of our moon sideswiped the Earth and exploded into an orbiting cloud of molten iron and debris. A metallic hailstorm ensued for many years, if not centuries, ripping atoms from water molecules and leaving hydrogen behind. The newly born oxygens were linked with iron, creating vast deposits of iron oxide across the planet's surface. The hydrogen formed a dense atmosphere that lasted an estimated 200 million years as it slowly dissipated into space.

After approximately forty million years of cooling, the planet became geologically active. Simple organic molecules began to form under the blanket of hydrogen. Those molecules eventually linked up to form RNA—a molecular player credited as essential for life's dawn. Then carbon, oxygen, hydrogen, nitrogen, phosphorus, and sulfur interacted in such a way that transformed them into life-bacteria, fungi, plants, and eventually prehistoric ape-like humans, and then our species of humans.

So here we stand, poised for yet another potent evolutionary leap of consciousness. But this time, it's not a sideswipe from a giant asteroid that sparks the change. It's you and me and the entire team of Soldiers of Love who are the spark that will create fire for the second time in human history.

Making a Living While Making a Difference

Today, the state of the world is anything but clear. Consequently, there has never been a more important time in history for people devoted to helping others. There has never been a greater need or greater opportunity for reward. Sharing knowledge and raising consciousness is a booming profession. The world truly needs and deserves all of the help we can provide.

People are sick, exhausted, angry, confused, and in desperate need of guidance and support. Many are lacking the basic skills to process the toxic political culture, CoVid-19, the layoffs, social distancing, and all of the fear-based propaganda combined with fear-based programs they picked up in childhood. They don't have the know-how or energy left to ward off stress and disease, let alone create a life of fulfillment.

Billions of people all over the world are searching the internet every day looking for answers and hoping for help. They are in need of *something* or *someone* to help them shift the trajectory of their lives. There are so many people in need that every teacher, every guide, every life coach on the planet could work 100 hours a week, and *still*, there would not be enough of us to take care of even ten percent of the need. (I might have made that up.) The point is that there are not enough of us to ever view each other as competition. Instead, we will be most successful when we work together as a team to transform this moment into something colossal, uniquely accessible, and incredibly effective.

By uniting and supporting each other to succeed, we amplify our ability to be a force for good. Whenever we have a student or client who doesn't feel in alignment, we can refer them to someone who is a better match. As we get crystal clear on who we want to serve, we also become better at saying no when we have niggling doubts or even red flags about taking on a client. In this way, we narrow our clients down to those who are the most perfect fit for us and repel those who are not a good fit.

Years ago I thought that I could help *anyone* transform and awaken to their true essence thereby allowing them to be more functional, joyful, and kind. I was wrong—very wrong. Misunderstandings, misinterpretations, and mismeasures are inevitable in any line of work. Those of us in the self-development industry are not immune to this, especially when there is not proper alignment. This can create conflict, suffering, and drama that cannot be remedied or repaired. When we work with those who are in proper alignment with us, there is understanding, harmony, trust, and respect. The point is that you want to spend your time and energy intentionally, efficiently, and wisely. When you have students and clients who are in alignment, you bring out the best in each other. When the alignment is missing, it often ends in conflict.

For this mission to be a movement and to make as much impact as humanly possible, we need to unite and rise above the static and noise and make a real difference. People like you and me who care enough to pull out all of the stops and take our mission to help people as far as humanly possible.

Deprogramming the Mind/Upgrading Your Blueprint

Systemic programming has programmed false beliefs into the hearts and minds of our global culture. This is programming that fools people into believing that they are inherently flawed and destined for suffering and eternal damnation. It's fear-based conditioning. Fear suppresses the immune system and feeds the idea that we are incapable of being healthy and happy without being saved by pharmaceuticals, politicians, or religious figures—without someone or something outside ourselves. Our mission is to awaken people from this nightmare and show them how to shed harmful and limiting programs and create new and empowering ones. Through modeling and teaching these principles and practices, we help people to become the best versions of themselves, all the while becoming the best version of ourselves.

We Are an Army of Love

I invite you to join this community of like-minded people who are committed to making the world a better place. We are an expanding community committed to bringing out the best in ourselves and each other with unconditional love and support. We hold ourselves to a high standard of behavior and enjoy a high quality of life. We are guides, coaches, teachers, healers, intuitives, counselors, therapists, doctors, yogis, martial artists, dakas, and dakinis on a sacred journey, committed to doing everything in our power to make this world a better place for all inhabitants.

You are needed, because you can add value and make a massive impact while reaping the benefits of being well-paid and leading the way for a better future. Making this commitment is not something to not be taken lightly. It's not like taking a magic pill. It is a path that we walk every moment of every day. It's a life-long commitment to doing what is right no matter what. It is beautiful work but—make no mistake about it—hard work and massive action are two of our greatest tools.

Because I dedicated myself to constantly learning and growing, I was led to a powerful combination of transformational tools that allowed me to first transform my life and then support others in doing the same. I have distilled this learning into an Evolutionary Blueprint made up of the core principles, practices, and qualities that have supported me in shifting from a path that was bound to end up in ruin to one of love and peace. Using this Blueprint you can wipe out outdated, fear-based programs and install new updated programs that enable you to be blessed with more love, laughter, and bliss. You can wake up your energy body, your potential, your inner Soldier of Love, and help wake up the world. Are you ready? Let's jump in!

"Be the change you wish to see in the world."
—Gandhi

"We teach best what we most want to learn."
—Richard Bach

Chapter 2

Your Evolutionary
Blueprint

In the quotes to the left, Gandhi is telling us we have to *be* what we seek to find outside of ourselves in order to get it. Richard Bach shares that what we are best at teaching is that which we have not yet mastered but deeply desire to learn. Both of these quotes are true! To put it succinctly, you must own everything you want to give away, and give away everything you want to own.

It starts with you, so you must become your own best student. Defining moments from your childhood shaped you in conscious and unconscious ways. You've been *programmed* by your life circumstances and by your caregivers. Most of this was done without conscious intent, which is why we all have warped ideas about who we are and what we can or can't do in the world. This programming becomes the *Blueprint* from which all of our beliefs and actions stem.

Most people have absolutely no idea how powerful and magical they truly are. They have been programmed to question, dislike, or even secretly (or not so secretly) loathe themselves. They have been programmed to believe they are powerless, alone, unworthy, sinful, or unlovable. Those who have been around the block a time or two in the self-development world may have an idea about these old programs that run around inside of our heads without our expressed permission. But, for many people, this is all going on in the background. Just like you don't think much about the programming happening behind the screen of your phone or laptop, most people don't think much about the unconscious programming sitting at the foundation of their self-concept.

Many people have been taught that human beings are spiritually wounded and have to be saved by a deity or preacher, prophet, or a set of beliefs. Others find a kind of "salvation" from the pain of their programming by "drowning their sorrows" in nicotine, caffeine, alcohol, street drugs, or prescription pharmaceuticals. Soldiers of Love reject the notion that we need to be saved by any outside source. We know that true power is within and everything that we need to be our best selves is within us now. Every desire comes with the means to actualize it. The real savior is inside every single one of us. All we need to do is access and upgrade the Blueprint we are working with to make profound changes to our self-concept and our life choices.

The most important key to understanding *how* to make our lives and the world better is the knowledge that there are only two major vibrations on this planet: Love and Fear. They are both incredibly magnetic and are constantly pulling people towards them. Every decision is an opportunity to choose love over fear.

Love is the healthiest and most pleasurable; fear is the exact opposite. When vibrating in fear, we are contracted, unhealthy, and unhappy. When we are vibrating in love, we are expanded, healthy, and joyful.

In spiritual circles, codependent families, or even tightly-knit social groups, sometimes people think that being loving means we can't have good boundaries or think about what is best for ourselves. That can lead to saying *yes* when what is needed is a strong *no*, or saying *no* when what we really want is to say *yes*. This is NOT love, as it is not loving toward the self. More importantly, it is often based on hidden fears that if we do what we know is right for us, someone will judge us, leave us, hurt us, or humiliate us.

Sometimes love needs to take a firm stand. And that can be hard.

Once we claim and embody our natural state, we can rid ourselves of the negative programs and limiting beliefs, allowing freedom and progress to reign. Programs get their power from the unconscious questions we ask all the time. We wonder which choice will get us the desired outcome—to be loved, safe, connected, empowered, in control, wealthy, winners. Some of these questions are healthy. Some are very unhealthy.

The quality of our lives is a direct reflection of the quality of the questions we are asking; they are the lines, measurements, and markings that make up our Blueprint.

These questions set off unconscious programs that are responsible for our pain and dysfunction. These programs need to be rewritten; our Blueprint needs upgrading. It's not as mysterious as it seems. We simply need to find the faulty or unhealthy questions and, with intention and attention, rewrite them to better align with our true essence. The same is true for our social systems, cultural norms, and institutions. They run on unconscious programming driven by questions, some healthy and some unhealthy. Here are a few examples:

- Imagine how different the health-care industry would be if it's underlying question was "How do we help people thrive and live a vibrant and fulfilling life?" rather than, "How do we avoid death?"
- Imagine how our schools would be different if the underlying question was, "How do we help children realize their full unique potential?" vs., "How do we prepare them for work?"

- Imagine how different our corporations would be if they asked "How do we help our employees live fulfilling lives while exceeding our customers' expectations?" instead of "How do we make a great profit this quarter and push up our stock prices?"

While it can seem overwhelming to try to change the underlying questions, it's important to remember that these organizations are made up of and run by people. The more people we can help to see and change the faulty questions and unhealthy programs that are running unconsciously, the faster we will see real, lasting change in our social structures.

If we are to save the world from fear, hate, ignorance, incompetence, and poverty by exposing and resolving the systemic, unconscious programming that creates suffering and dysfunction, we must both seek to conquer those things within ourselves, and seek to support others in doing the same. Fortunately, we have the help of the greatest communication tool ever created: the internet. Now we can learn anything, anywhere, from anyone in the world. And you can teach anything to anyone from anywhere in the world!

Creating and selling online courses is a booming industry internationally. The e-learning market was estimated to be worth $107 billion in 2015, $190 billion in 2018 and is expected to exceed $300 billion by 2025—and those are pre-CoVid numbers. People are streaming audiobooks, podcasts, documentaries, and online courses more than at any other time in history, and with the pandemic keeping more people at home than ever before, this is growing exponentially. Not only is the technology and desire for content exploding, but our audience is also riper for personal and spiritual transformation than ever before. If you consider yourself spiritual but not religious, you are far from alone. It is estimated that 27 percent of all Americans eighteen years old and above now say that they are spiritual but not religious. That is more than 56 million Americans who are searching for answers that make sense. And the spiritual but not religious group is by far the fastest-growing segment of the United States population.

In addition to that 27 percent, another 48 percent say that they are both religious and spiritual. To me, this means they have more open minds than those who say they are religious but not spiritual or say they are neither. *This* is your audience; *these* are your people. And they are waiting for you to come out of hiding and offer your story, your experience, your ideas, your wisdom, and your genius so that they can follow along behind you, or walk beside you, as we evolve together into our most magical and powerful selves.

Are you ready and willing to step forward now as a Soldier of Love and embody within yourself the change we wish to see, and guide and support others in making that same change? Are you ready and willing to make a great living while doing it?

The next pages will lay out the seven sacred virtues that form the Evolutionary Blueprint. By cultivating these ideals, I have helped thousands of clients come home to magnificence within themselves, have built a successful and lucrative business, and I have helped many others use these principles to do the same. It gives me great pleasure to share them with you as a fellow Soldier of Love. *Onward!*

Your Evolutionary Blueprint Overview

By aligning with the laws of nature we amplify and enhance our abilities while becoming happier, healthier leaders. The most fundamental law of all is this: what continues to grow continues to survive and thrive and what does not grow ceases to thrive and survive. Or put more simply: *grow or die.*

For our community to do the best work possible, we must have a conscious relationship with our own Blueprint and some capacity to redesign it when we discover it is off. The following commitments form the foundation for the Evolutionary Blueprint. These commitments guide us as we go along the journey and remind us of why we are here and what we are about.

Soldiers of Love are committed to:

- Making the world a better place while thoroughly enjoying the process
- Being a shining example by becoming the best version of ourselves
- Having a daily personal empowerment practice to regularly upgrade our Evolutionary Blueprint
- Helping people to be the best versions of themselves through modeling, guiding, and teaching the skills required to experience and inspire true transformation
- Training with passionate, transformational teachers and guides from all walks of life
- Teaching the game-changing courses and masterminds online and in-person
- Writing books, articles, and blogs that provide inspiration and education to readers
- Speaking to audiences, small and large, in ways that are impactful, fun, and lucrative
- Holding a vision of educating and empowering millions

Now that we are clear about what we are committing to, we can begin exploring the seven sacred principles that will help us meet and exceed these commitments:

1. Cultivating Presence

2. Mastering Energy

3. Living in Balance

4. Developing Discipline

5. Creating Clarity

6. Acquiring Skills

7. Taking Action

1. Cultivating Presence

Studies have shown that an average person is fully present to what is happening in the current moment less than 10 percent of the time. In fact, one study indicated that 94 to 99 percent of waking hours people are thinking about the past or the future, not the present. Most of those thoughts were worries, concerns, or regrets. Quite often the same thoughts get caught in a loop like a broken record going round and round. The human body is designed to be inhabited fully by a person's energy and intention. However, the many distractions of life are in our hands most of the day. On our cell phones, we stay connected to social media platforms like Twitter, Instagram, Facebook, Snapchat, and now TikTok. The pull can be overwhelming, and it is damaging our ability to stay in the present.

Cultivating Presence is a critical skill for a Soldier of Love because all the magic happens in the present moment. When people learn the skill of Presence, it affects every aspect of their lives. When we are not fully present, it is like we are on autopilot. We might get to where we intend to go, but we are deprived of an intentionally designed and quality experience on the journey. This chapter shares powerful techniques for breaking the habit of non-attention and cultivating the kind of Presence that allows you to see opportunities for healing, prosperity, connection, and love that others miss. It's a game-changer!

2. Mastering Energy

Everything in our universe is made up of frequencies of light carrying information. Our most precious commodity is energy. When we feel energetic, we handle ourselves and our lives with a sense of enthusiasm and vigor. When energy is lacking, we feel sluggish and down. When a body runs out of energy, it instantly perishes. This is why energy is our most precious resource. Understanding this, Soldiers of Love understand and master the skills necessary to manage their energy body.

Many of the techniques I teach my students are a combination of ancient lineages and art forms, including but not limited to martial arts, qi gong, Tantra, Taoism, and indigenous energy practices. I also bring in modern understandings from quantum science and neuroscience. These practices can put you into a state of presence, power, clarity, and balance. Through guided meditations, I will teach you the most important practices I know to help you master your energy.

3. Living in Balance

In my travels, I have had the pleasure of meeting many wonderful people. I have met dozens of medicine men and women with incredible talents and exceptional skills who didn't have balance; therefore, they never reached their full potential. Not reaching one's full potential not only means sub-par financial success but also means not having the greatest reach or the most potent impact in their chosen field of service. This is a huge loss for everyone. Sometimes it's just a matter of hidden beliefs or outdated blueprints that impede their ability to attain a clear perspective.

A common misconception that blocks people from being as financially abundant as they would like to be is the belief that being well paid for helping people is somehow not spiritual. I reject that notion and embrace the principle of fluent and efficient flow of energy. The more value you provide, the more you should be compensated. The more you give, the more flow will return to you. But you must be in alignment with that reality to make it so. On the opposite end of the spectrum, people in the helping professions consistently over-give to the point of giving out. Their physical health suffers, their relationships are in turmoil, and it never seems like they are doing enough.

This chapter explores how to serve others while not losing yourself. It seems like such a simple concept, but it is very challenging to maintain when you are passionate about being of service. I will share my struggle to maintain balance as a successful daka and some of the cosmic head-butts I needed to restore balance to my life.

4. Developing Discipline

A Soldier of Love is only as effective as the amount of discipline he has. It's a common misperception that you either have it or you don't. Discipline is a skill set that needs to be practiced daily. It needs to be developed and then mastered. Without discipline, you have no follow-through, and without follow-through, we cannot be a Soldier of Love in the fight to evolve ourselves and our world. This chapter shares some key concepts that have helped my students and me to develop the discipline that it takes to make a real difference in the world.

5. Creating Clarity

Few things in life can bring about the downfall of what we hold dear than a lack of clarity. Confusion is a natural precursor to learning. At Tony Robbins seminars when someone raises their hand and says they are confused, we cheer because it means they are about to learn something. However, being in battle without a battle plan is a recipe for disaster. No nation prospers without a shared vision and mission around which to rally. No road trip goes well without a map to the destination.

Consider how much more efficiently we arrive at our destination when we know where we are going. Before we had GPS systems built into our vehicles and cell phones, people would often find themselves driving around lost. I remember this being a commonly shared joke. The men wouldn't listen to their wives, and then they would get lost, eventually pulling over to ask a stranger for guidance. Now we type or speak the address and go straight to our destination. Think of the staggering amount of energy that can be saved if we take time to create clarity.

This chapter examines the lenses through which we view ourselves and our world around us. We will bring into focus your unique essence as a guiding principle. And we will examine how judgment can cloud the picture. Once we can clear our perceptions, we will do the vital work of defining our life's mission. To successfully bring forth a healed inner and outer world, a Soldier of Love needs a clear mission.

6. Acquiring Skills

A Soldier of Love must be devoted to self-mastery and committed to making the world a better place by being an example of someone who spreads massive amounts of love and joy to as many people as possible through teaching. To rise to this mission, we will need to have a set of skills to master life and then the desire and willingness to share those tools with other human beings. Together we will raise the consciousness on the planet and create more competent and joyful human beings.

In short, a Soldier of Love must walk the talk. You will set an example for others by investing time and energy into your self-care so that when you teach others to do the same, you can do it from a place of authenticity and experience. This chapter explores the underlying concepts of acquiring skills, including developing focus and mindfulness, understanding the four stages of learning, and finding your unique voice in the world.

7. Taking Action

It won't matter how well you have developed yourself or how many skills you acquire if you are unable to put your vision for a new self and a new world into action. This is one of the challenges of spiritual teachings. Often they feel more at home on the yoga mat or meditation cushion than out in the "real world." But as Soldiers of Love, we have a responsibility to do more than think about what we want to change inside and outside of ourselves, we must bring it forth in the material world. This chapter introduces strategies for moving past our blocks to taking action. We will also look at the importance of accountability and how the habit of inaction can sabotage our best designs. Finally, we will bring everything together into a clear vision for the future.

This book is filled with powerful exercises that will help you build your Evolutionary Blueprint so you can be the most high-functioning version of yourself. I have created a workbook and audio meditations to help you do the exercises. You can access them for free at **SoldierofLoveWorkbook.com**. Please download and print the workbook and use the audio files where guided throughout this book. This will greatly enhance your experience.

"Few delights can equal the mere presence of one whom we trust utterly."

—George MacDonald

"Shrinking in a corner, pressed into the wall; do they know I'm present, am I here at all?"

—Lang Leav

Chapter 3

CULTIVATING PRESENCE

When my mother was pregnant with me, she was thrown down a flight of stairs. We know that fetuses in the womb can hear and respond to voices, emotions, and energy. They most certainly are impacted by violence. When my mother was attacked in this way, it caused my nervous system's fight/flight response to engage, and from then on, I was basically in survival mode. As early as I can remember, I had so much adrenaline flowing through my veins that I struggled to sit still. I was ready for a fight anytime it was needed, and I had to work hard to control my anger. Becoming a highly skilled athlete helped, but I was over-amped much of the time.

About sixteen years ago, I received a special kind of energy healing session called "reaching" from my friend and teacher Lynda Ceasara that shifted my nervous system and turned off my fatigued adrenal glands. My nervous system had been stuck in sympathetic/ action mode for most of my life. After that healing session, I felt more calm and content than I ever had. Even though I had been studying personal growth since the 1980s and was already an advanced certified Tantra Yogi who meditated and did the practices necessary to achieve inner calm, it was an energetic reboot that completely upgraded my ability to function optimally.

I continued to study with Lynda for the next fifteen years and eventually taught with her for the last five of those years. Everything I learned and shared with others was designed to cultivate presence. Each new technique allowed me to master more of myself. Without knowing these powerful techniques for mastering and managing my energy body, I would have continued to have to work extremely hard at controlling my anger and reactivity when triggered.

Presence is the opposite of being triggered. It's being in awareness from your natural state of balance, clarity, and deep attention. Only in the present moment can we tap into our body's innate intelligence and miraculous internal guidance system. The human body's capabilities, when fully present, are truly stunning.

How to Be Present in the Moment

I think it's fair to say that most people have had the experience of speaking to someone who seems like they are elsewhere. It is impossible to be fully present if you're thinking about what you need to accomplish in the future. It is also impossible to be fully present if you're thinking about things that happened in the past. Many of us are so used to living in the past or the future that we have no awareness of what being in the present means. Recent research has shown that we are not as conscious as we think we are. In fact, we are unconscious most of the time as we move about our day, with only specific decisions making their way into our consciousness. Because of this, we struggle to live in the present. Our mind swings from thought to thought, only briefly settling somewhere that captures our truest form of attention. To become more mindful and present in your life, focus on these three areas:

1. Unselfconsciousness

Thinking about yourself and how you appear to others takes you out of the moment. When you are in a situation where you already feel anxious, focusing on the anxiety only worsens it. Instead of focusing on what's going on in your head, feel into what is happening around you and how you are a part of that. Mindfulness blurs the line that exists between yourself and others. Without feelings of self-consciousness, you can witness the feeling or perception of being evaluated by others without feeling threatened and taking it personally.

2. Savoring

Being so caught up in our thoughts prevents us from truly experiencing and enjoying our own lives. Instead of appreciating what we're experiencing, we think of when the next time we'll get to share this again is or how the experience could be better. Learning how to direct your attention allows you to become an expert at savoring the present moment. No matter what the moment is, note how you're feeling in all of your senses. Taking a few extra minutes to savor daily activities helps you feel more joy and happiness and experience fewer depressive symptoms. Savor the taste of food, rather than gulping it down. Savor the feeling of fresh air as you walk to your car rather than replaying what happened in your meeting. Savor the smell of your favorite cologne, perfume, or lotion to bring yourself into the moment. Because most negative thoughts involve the past or future, being present forces you to stop ruminating on the past and stop catastrophizing about the future.

3. Acceptance

When faced with pain or discomfort, our natural reaction is to avoid it. Resisting unpleasant feelings and thoughts means that you don't have to face them. Humans have two types of emotions: primary and secondary. Secondary emotions are ones that we feel around other feelings. When we feel stressed out about being busy at work, the primary emotion is the stress surrounding your workload, and the secondary emotion is hating feeling stressed. Instead of fighting these emotions, allow yourself to take them in. Be open to how you feel in the present moment without judging your feelings or trying to push them away. Focusing on your secondary emotions instead of feeling your primary ones actually prolongs the negative feelings. Accepting these emotions doesn't mean you like them and want to feel this way forever. Instead, it means that you don't resist where you are in the moment, knowing it will eventually pass.

Applying these three techniques will help you develop presence. When you are present for each situation in your life, whether at work, in your relationship with your partner, or when hanging out with friends, the quality of your life experience will dramatically increase. And, it is essential when working with clients.

The present moment is where all the magic happens. People can connect most deeply when they're fully present. People are stronger, healthier, and happier when they learn how to be present. Why? Because being present helps us to see ourselves and others clearly. It helps us to notice the places where we may need to grow and evolve. This is critical if we are to serve as a Soldier of Love, here to help evolve our communities and our planet. We cannot give away what we don't have ourselves.

If we want the world to evolve, we must also be committed to our own evolution.

One of the first things we need to do is notice which old childhood patterns of behavior and thought hold us back. It's as if we were given our basic programming as kids, and now as adults, it's time for an upgrade.

Breaking Free from Old Programming

The quality of your life is a result of the decisions that you make regularly. The decisions that you make are a direct reflection of the quality of questions that you ask. Most people are not aware that they are asking themselves and the world questions all the time. The deepest, subconscious question that we all need to be answered is, "How can I be/feel safe?"

Unfortunately, when the question is unconscious, the answers we give ourselves aren't always the best answers. Because we aim to have the very best experience of life, we want to begin directing the questions we ask and catching ourselves when we are operating unconsciously. Making the shift from asking, "How can I be/feel safe?" to "How can I thrive?" is a big step forward. These unconscious and habitual questions are just like the programs that run your computer. Programs are run on algorithms. Algorithms are simply questions put into mathematical equations. And just like computer programs, *our behavioral programs are upgradable.*

A Soldier of Love takes advantage of this by seeking to upgrade their internal programming continually. You recognize this need and, even as you read this book, are evolving yourself. Of course, until we die, our evolutionary journey is still unfolding.

We will look at some other ways to continue your evolution, starting by doing a short analysis of your programming.

With a clean sheet of paper or a new document open, jot down the following questions. Then set aside some committed time to answer them with your full attention:

- What are the areas in your life that you struggle with?
- What are the areas of your life that are easy?
- Select the top three areas of your life that most urgently need improvement.
- What types of improvements have you attempted to make in each of these areas? How pleased are you with the results?

- What has held you back from making improvements in those areas?
- Describe in detail what each of these areas looks like if you have them functioning optimally for you.

More About Programming

It's no secret that our past experiences can create a skewed perception of life. Past experiences that have caused pain or confusion tend to stay with us and become part of our identity, making being present extremely difficult. When stuck in a thinking loop, or trying to make sense of today through the lens of a past experience, it is impossible to tap into your body's natural intelligence by being present. Generally speaking, the programming of human beings mostly happens in early childhood. Governments, religious organizations, school structures, the media, and corporate politics are not immune to passing down fear-based programs that damage our sense of self. These programs are riddled with bugs and glitches, or misalignments and problems, that keep us from functioning at our highest level. Most of what we learn is faulty in some way.

One of the most prevalent faulty programs that humans run is the illusion that they are simply not enough. Not good-looking enough, not rich enough, not smart enough, not tall enough, not fit enough, not dark enough, not light enough, not worthy enough to (fill in the blank). I reject these programs with all my heart. Humans are miraculous beings, born with the capacity to meet their dreams and desires. However, to experience the depth of how miraculous we are, we need to learn how to be in the present moment.

To be happy and fulfilled, the first task is to clear our perceptions and rid ourselves of the programming that keeps us believing that we are not enough or that we need someone or something to complete us. We do not need a savior to come from the outside. Our true savior is within us. Within every person is the ability to fulfill all their desires. Within every desire comes the mechanisms to achieve it and attain it. We need to get clear on what we desire, put that desire into an intention, and create a new program.

Time for an Upgrade

As a Soldier of Love, you need to upgrade your program to one that purges all that unnecessary self-loathing and self-doubt. You need programming that allows you to spend more time vibrating in the energy of love and less in self-criticism. Self-criticism leads to paralysis—and there's no time for that in this "all hands on deck" moment. You need programming that allows you to be the happiest and most successful version of yourself that you have ever imagined—the version that will bring more love and joy not only to yourself but to others. Let's get started with the re-programming process.

Building Your Blueprint Exercise

Remember, to help you build your Blueprint, access the free Soldier of Love Workbook at **SoldierofLoveWorkbook.com**.

1) Make a list of the top ten things that you would change about your life. These might be things like your working situation, your living situation, income, friends, or relationships.

2) Make a list of the top ten things that you want to change about yourself. This is a list of qualities you have or don't have, not material things or things outside of yourself like the first list. Imagine you could snap your fingers and transform three things about your personality. What would they be? Do you wish you had more patience, better boundaries, less judgment?

3) Review your list and rewrite any items stated in the negative so that the list takes you from where you are to where you want to go. Make sure that anything you don't want to do has been expanded to include what you want to do instead. Example: *Stop procrastinating* gets expanded to *Stops procrastinating and take decisive action on my top priorities.*

Building Your Blueprint: Activate Your Core Code

Once you have your list and you have expanded as needed, you can create your "Core Code." Your Core Code is what I refer to as a guiding light that can inspire you and hold you accountable. It's your Core Code that keeps you on track so that you can fulfill your destiny as a Soldier of Love.

My Core Code is something I carry with me and keep in my wallet at all times. When I start experiencing emotions and urges that are not aligned with who I want to be, I refer to my future-self program. Now truth be told, your Core Code does not necessarily have to be 100 percent attainable. Mine is not. My Core Code includes a desire to be perfect, but as we know, human beings are only perfect in our essence. Behaviorally, we make a lot of mistakes. This aim for perfection works for me, primarily because I run a pattern that likes the idea of perfection (more on that in the next chapter). For you, the idea of perfection may be overwhelming or demotivating. No problem. The idea is to design a Core Code that works with your needs.

Keep in mind that this new program is not meant to be something to compare yourself to that makes you feel bad. It is merely something to strive for, a kind of "True North" that helps you stay focused and reorient when you find yourself out of alignment. For example, if you struggle with a lack of discipline, you want to create a Core Code where you see yourself as a person who operates in disciplined ways with ease. Suppose you also want to shift away from having a quick temper and inability to listen. In that case, you create your Core Code to include being a great listener with all the tools and techniques needed so that the quick-triggered temper does not manifest in your behavior.

Once you have all the elements of your future self fleshed out, capture this vision in various ways. Here are some options:

- Make a high-level bulleted list with words that cue you to shift into your Core Code.
- Write out a new story for your life, imagined in great detail.
- Create a "Perfect Day" journal entry that allows you to see your Core Code in action.
- Collect images online and paste them into a document that illustrates the feel and quality of your Core Code.
- Write a poem or song that captures your Core Code.
- Make a playlist of music that helps you connect with the feelings and qualities of your future self.
- Draw or paint a portrait of yourself with your Core Code fully activated and online, or hire a freelancer on Fiverr.com or another platform to do it for you.
- Create a special place in your home where you sit and meditate on the qualities and feelings of your Core Code.
- Dedicate a section of your closet to the kinds of clothes that you will wear when you have achieved your Core Code and begin letting go of those items you wouldn't wear when you have achieved your Core Code.
- Look around your home and release anything that doesn't align with your Core Code.
- Place a reminder of your Core Code on your bathroom mirror.

- Read your list of Core Code qualities before bed or after rising to help you tune into yourself when living from your Core Code.

In short, make time to define deeply and then envision precisely who you want to be and commit to being that person more and more each day.

Self-Referencing and Other-Referencing

The final element of mastering your energy is minimizing the influence of others on your energy field. In some cases, this influence is unwanted and unconscious. In other cases, we may feel unsure of ourselves or lack confidence, so we seek validation from outside of ourselves. It is not unusual for people who grew up with very opinionated or controlling caregivers, or who were in partnerships with controlling people, to find themselves constantly checking in with others to figure out how they are supposed to feel. This is called "other-referencing."

We other-reference when we have not developed a strong enough relationship with ourselves to measure what it is we want, need, or desire in any given situation. Or we may know what it is, but dismiss it because we have measured others and decided (with or without evidence) that they will be hurt or angered by our need, want, or desire. Alternately, self-referencing is an effective form of measuring based on cues and responses from your own body. Other-referencing is sub-optimal. Self-referencing is optimal. Unfortunately, most people are not self-referencing most of the time.

To self-reference, one must be fully present, centered, and in their core. For example, if I have a craving for a piece of chocolate cake, I may ask myself the questions, "Is this going to be worth it? Is this piece of cake going to give me enough pleasure to compensate for the sugar and carbs that I will be putting in my body?" For me, my proper self-referencing will return an answer of, "*Hell*, no." This doesn't mean that I won't occasionally have a piece of cake anyway. However, when I do have it, I know that I'm making an exception with the full understanding that it is going against my healthy mindset.

If I were making the decision to eat the cake by other-referencing, it would look like this. I would weigh my desire to eat the cake against what I think others would say or think about me. For example, I want to have a piece of cake, but I see other people watching me, and I believe that they are judging me. Consequently, I make my decision based on how my actions might look to others. I might choose to eat it anyway as a way of proving I am not controlled by their judgments (which I may or may not have evidence for), but I am still deciding as a reaction to them.

Of course, the stakes are usually much higher than eating a piece of cake. In the worst-case scenarios, those who other-reference may base their sense of worth on what other people say or do, even on how many likes they get on social media. When people other-reference on a regular basis, it becomes an unconscious habit in which they tend to ignore their body's natural intelligence, which leads to decisions that are not in the best interest of their health, happiness, productivity, or their general sense of fulfillment.

Exercises for Cultivating Presence

1) Use this simple exercise whenever you catch yourself or anyone else checking out of a conversion: Clamp your hands and stomp your feet playfully and say, "Come back to the present moment!" When practiced regularly, this fun little pattern-interrupt can truly help you learn to break the habit of zoning out. I know it may feel silly. That's why it

actually works! The novel experience and slight discomfort of the action with speaking the mantra out loud allow your mind to come back to now and stay engaged. Have fun with it and remember to do it every time you catch yourself not being present.

2) The best way to stay present is to master your energy. The next chapter includes an Essentials meditation with key practices to help you physically embody Presence. Use the Essentials meditation daily in the next chapter for 45 days to give you an embodied experience of being fully present, in your core, taking up space, and supported by the universal forces of the Earth and the sun. And from now on, commit to having your essentials in place before you make a decision of any kind. Just give yourself a moment to make sure you are grounded, centered, shielded, and cleared. When you make a decision from this place, you will be able to ask your body for an answer and measure from your core.

Remember that you can't accurately manage anything unless you can effectively measure it. To manage your life, your decisions, and your relationships, it is critical to develop *self*-referencing skills rather than *other*-referencing. Being present will naturally lead you into a relationship with your energy body and how well you are or not able to manage it. The next chapter explores the fundamental concepts necessary to truly understand your energy body and how you move (or don't move) energy through your system. You will learn how to ground your energy, clear your energy, and strengthen your vibration and your unique frequency. And you will learn how to be more masterful with your attention and intention.

"Energy cannot be created or destroyed. Only changed from one form to another."

—Albert Einstein

Chapter 4

MASTERING ENERGY

Energy is our most precious commodity. Without enough energy, all the money, fame, and time in the world means very little. Energy can neither be created nor destroyed, but it can be enhanced, amplified, or depleted. Because energy is, for the most part, an unseen force, many people have a hard time believing that they have any control over it. Science is still seeking to understand energy to its fullest extent. However, there are some things we can use to inform us about how energy behaves so that we can have a better chance of directing it.

Our universe and everything in it is made out of subatomic particles. These subatomic particles are mostly vast spaces with a defined edge: 99 percent space, to be exact. Think of it as a cell with lots of space circled by its intelligent membrane just like the earth, which is an electromagnetic energy field with an atmosphere (a defined edge) that keeps us safe from all manner of harmful penetration of meteors and other types of space junk.

We are also made up of billions of these energized subatomic particles with energy fields ringed by an edge. A fascinating fact is that these fields can hold and transfer vast amounts of information such as light, heat, movement, and density. All of this, and more, provides clues that can be seen and understood. These frequencies are simply light carrying information.

The fundamental understanding in physics, known as the Conservation of Energy, states that the energy within a system remains constant: energy can't be created or destroyed. Energy is an incredibly important concept to understand because it is the basic building block of life. For this discussion, we need to realize that everything in the universe is made up of microscopic, subatomic particles. You can imagine them as sparks of light that are surrounded by massive amounts of space. Deepak Chopra says, "If you had one grain of sand and you were to float it in the center of the Sistine Chapel, you would see the difference between what is solid and what is space in all of our cells."

Despite appearances, very little of us is solid; perhaps 1 percent of our body is solid, 99 percent is space, and in that, 75 percent of us is water. We are made out of the same stuff as our pets, dishes, cars, and everything else in the universe. Under a microscope, subatomic particles look identical. The particles can vary in the amount of space they have around them and how they are stacked. For example, with enough pressure (or change in space and stacking), a piece of coal can turn into a diamond. A diamond will be tougher; it can cut through more things but has less space and less consciousness. In our world, diamonds have been deemed more valuable than any other kind of stone, but they have less energy from an energetic perspective, and perhaps less consciousness, than a rock.

We have so much more space in us than the rock or diamond. Under pressure, we too can contract. The edge of our field can get beaten down. If we allow our fields to become small and weak, we will go on not being noticed and not making a difference. With people, the contraction comes from fear-based behavior and disempowering thoughts or experiences that make our edge get weaker and smaller, which makes us less powerful, less productive, less effective, and less celebratory. Less able to have a positive impact on the world.

As a Soldier of Love who is cultivating Presence, you have learned to eliminate old and unhelpful programming in your thoughts. At the energetic level, we can learn how to consciously create a more positive, more useful energetic state to support staying present.

Understanding Your Energy Anatomy

The energy body is a complex, highly intelligent field that has many layers. In the yogic tradition, there are layers to the energy body. Encased by the physical sheath, interpenetrating it and transcending it are the three layers of the subtle body: the *pranamaya kosha,* or vital energy sheath; the *manomaya kosha,* or mental sheath; and the *vijnanamaya kosha,* or wisdom sheath. According to ancient Eastern wisdom, these layers are sometimes known as *koshas.* These layers may include the physical or gross body, the energy or subtle body, the mental body, the spiritual body, the emotional body, and the causal body (before form.)

Pretty much all the yogic traditions talk about the energy body and its energetic pathways, called *meridians, chakras*, and *nadis*. These energetic pathways allow life force energy, also known as *shakti* or *prana*, to move within our system. Think of the flow of energy like the flow of traffic. All the energy pathways are streets. These streets meet at a roundabout. The roundabouts have circular movements with incoming and outgoing roads. The circular motion of these roundabouts gives you an idea of how the chakras operate. The word chakra means *"wheel"* in Sanskrit. The idea is to do all you can to consciously keep your energy moving and circulating so that you can stay happy and healthy.

When I work with energy, I picture it appearing as water, only much more subtle. Like water, energy needs to keep moving to avoid stagnating and becoming infected or contaminated. Energy should be kept fresh. To keep the energy fresh in the body, take deep breaths with the visualization of emptying all the old air and energy out of the lungs and inhaling new clean, fresh, and vitalized energy.

The seven major body chakras are crucial components of the entire energy body. There are fourteen major chakras in all: seven in the body and seven outside of the body. For now, we will focus on those inside the body. Each of the seven body chakras governs the body's corresponding area, which includes the muscles and organs. Chakras are disc-like energetic intersections that emulate from bundles of nerve ganglia up and down the spine. When they are healthy and balanced, they spin in a circular motion. Much like eddies in a moving river, the energy can get stuck and turn stagnant, causing dysfunction. Chakras can also be out of alignment, manifesting in over- or under-expression.

Each chakra relates to a different set of physiological and psychological characteristics. When you develop an understanding of each chakra's traits, you are better able to track and resolve imbalances in the chakras before any long-term damage is done.

There are many simple practices you can do to bring your chakras, and your energy body as a whole, into balance. These include sets of yoga postures, meditations, and *pranayama* (breathing) exercises.

The base chakra or root chakra. In Sanskrit, it is called *Muladhara*. It is located at the base of the spine and governs the pelvic floor muscles, among others. The base chakra has to do with our sense of certainty, security, stability, and safety. Its element is earth.

The sacral chakra. In Sanskrit, it is called *Svadhisthana*. It has to do with creativity, sexuality, sensuality, variety, and adventure. It is located just below the navel, and its element is water.

The solar plexus chakra or power chakra is called *Manipura* in Sanskrit. It is located in the upper abdomen. This chakra has to do with our sense of significance and empowerment. Its element is fire.

The heart chakra. In Sanskrit, it is called *Anahata*. It is located in the center of the chest. The focus of this chakra is love and connection, and its element is air.

The throat or sound chakra. In Sanskrit, it is called *Vishuddha*. It is located in the throat area and has to do with spiritual input and spiritual output, as well as communication and expression of needs and desires. Its element is aether.

The third eye chakra. In Sanskrit, it is called *Ajna*. It is located in the center of the forehead between the eyebrows. This chakra has to do with insight, intuition, and clarity of mind. It governs the master-gland, which in turn governs millions of other glands in the body. This chakra has no element.

The crown chakra, or *Sahasrara* in Sanskrit. This chakra is located at the crown or top of the head, where you would literally wear a crown. This chakra has to do with your connection to your higher self, ascension, and spiritual transcendence. This chakra also has no element.

There are many excellent books and programs about the body's chakras, and I encourage you to deepen your understanding of these energy centers through yoga, meditation, and energy practices. My favorite way to work with and balance the chakras is with essential oils, specifically Bloom Fine Egyptian oils. Alabaster tablets with circular divots for holding precious oils related to each of the seven chakras have been found in the tombs of Pharaohs and High Priests dating back as far as 3,000 years. There is conclusive evidence that these oils were used in high ceremonies to invoke more elevated states of consciousness.

I learned about these oils from my studies with a master teacher on my travels to Egypt. I will share more with you about Gamal and the extraordinary experiences I have had with him later in the book. For now, it is enough to know that he comes from a long line of spiritual devotees who are part of the ancient Egyptian mystery school traditions. He is a fifth-generation alchemist whose family has been working with essential oils for hundreds of years. I have found that when I add these oils to my energy work, my clients experience potent shifts easily and quickly. These oils are best used to balance each of the chakras: Red Amber for Root/Base; Musk for Sacral; Jasmine for Solar Plexus; Rose for Heart; Amber Cashmere for Throat; Sandalwood for Third Eye; and Blue Lotus for Crown. In advanced studies, there are also oils for the seven non-body chakras.

Energetic Habits of Attention

Because this energy is a form of consciousness, we can interact with it and program it consciously or unconsciously. Just like there are membranes around your cells, and edges around the particles that make up your cells, your energy field has an edge. Becoming aware of your edge is a crucial part of becoming empowered and optimizing your energy and talents. Your edge is a powerful tool if you consciously choose to make it so. Our edges take orders from something; the question is, "What is that something?" Rather than allowing your field to take orders from prior programming or other people, your most optimal functioning comes from you taking full responsibility for your energy.

High-Functioning vs. Low-Functioning Field

A high-functioning field is a strong field. When your field is strong, you will be in your power. You will feel centered, balanced, and content. You are adaptable, able to handle anything thrown at you, and process experiences, energy, and information quickly and efficiently. A low-functioning field is a weak field. If your field is weak, you will feel disempowered, out of balance, discontent, rigid, and argumentative. You may notice that your thinking gets repetitive or stuck in loops or traps that you can't seem to stay out of. You will find you are unable to get your needs met or unable to adapt to change. When your field is weak, you may notice yourself seeking to blame, deflect, and avoid taking personal responsibility. If you find yourself spending more time than you want to in disputes with others, complaining, justifying, or worrying, that's a great indication that you have some work to do to bring yourself into a place of energy mastery.

As a Soldier of Love, you need to have enough mastery over your energy body so that you can modulate your voice. You also need masterful communication skills (which we will go into more deeply in Chapter 6) to express yourself clearly when owning your wants, needs, boundaries, fears, and desires. Uplevel your ability to communicate, be clear and concise, and speak your truth from a place of love. You will have the ability to stand in your power and take personal responsibility for the experiences in your life.

In my twenties, I spent a good amount of time hanging out at the bar where my buddy Joel was the deejay. One night, two guys started a fight with me. We took it out to the parking lot, where I essentially kicked their asses. When I came back in, I asked Joel, "Why do you think that people are always starting fights with me? Is there something about my energy that says, 'I want to fight?'"

"No," he replied. "But there is something about your energy that says, 'Go ahead test me, I dare you.'"

"That's not how I want to be seen," I said. "I want people to want to be my friend."

I went back outside and shook my body, vigorously for a good while. I connected with the adrenaline that was flowing through my body and imagined it going into the earth. I imagined making an internal adjustment that released whatever it was that was getting me into fights. I no longer wanted that to be any part of me. I kept on until I felt a kind of release in my body. When I came back in, Joel confirmed that something seemed different. This one experience had a huge impact. After that, I made more friends and only got into fights when I was protecting someone.

It is essential to learn to use your power of choice to direct your energy and show up how you choose. You can also focus your attention and consciously decide how much time you spend happy or miserable, attracting or repelling what you want. Most people have this awareness intuitively. However, what people do not typically realize is how much power we have in influencing our own energy and the energy of those around us. Just like your home, your body will shut down when overloaded. Our homes are equipped with circuit breakers that will flip to "off" if they are overloaded. Our body does the same thing. Being fatigued, low on sleep, and stressed not only robs us of our energy but decreases our capacity to handle what life sends our way.

The human body ceases to function correctly when attempting to hold anything that exceeds its current capacity. It's as though we are hanging out right on the edge of our capacity, and our circuit-breakers are constantly flipping. When we try to hold too much energy, we can short circuit the body's natural potential. When the energy body gets overloaded, the person feels triggered. There is too much energy to hold, and it has to be off-loaded. Interestingly, this isn't done in some random way. Because our bodies are electromagnetic energy fields, it appears that energy is off-loaded in predictable ways, or patterns, through openings in the structures of our fields.

The Reichian Energy Patterns

People use five primary patterns to help themselves move energy out of their systems when it gets to be too much to tolerate. These patterns were discovered and explained by Wilhelm Reich, who is considered the father of body-mind psychotherapy in the Western world. He was able to link psychological motivations and their resulting behaviors to the way people moved the energy in their bodies.

These patterns arise from our early experiences of relating and attaching to others. When these attempts at attachment are thwarted or subjected to traumatizing events, the way our body responds gets wired into our neural firing patterns, which then are repeated and recreated as adults. Over time, this way of moving energy becomes habituated and forms energetic habits of attention.

Because the energy gets moved over and over in the same way, it impacts the body's physical development. Since form follows energy, our posture, fatty deposits, musculature, and even organ functioning can be affected. For example, Reich observed that those who hold their energy in narrow channels tend to be physically narrower. Those who push their energy downward tend to be physically smaller in stature. In addition, we take on mental and emotional "armor" or adaptations that provide defense for us as we move through life. Reich called this *Characterology*.

As a Soldier of Love, we want to be conscious of our own patterns of moving energy as well as those of others. We need to know the pitfalls and gifts of each and what will allow us to move out of a coping pattern and move back into Presence. The following is a short introduction to these patterns.

The Schizoid Pattern

To understand this pattern imagine a flock of birds in a tree when suddenly a car backfires loudly, startling the birds, which then fly out frantically in all directions. This is similar to how somebody who runs the Schizoid (schiz) pattern leaves their body.

People who run the schiz pattern have come to rely on leaving their body in moments of overwhelm as a way to feel safe. They likely developed this pattern very early in life. By abandoning their body, they found a kind of peace as they separated from a source of pain. This action and the resulting fragmentation is a response to repeated shocks to the system and energetic and physical traumas that made being in the body feel unsafe. Like all of the Reichian energy patterns, for the person running the schiz pattern, leaving the body as a coping strategy became a habit. This habit can create a kind of pathway so that people using this strategy can seem easily overwhelmed.

The gift of this pattern is that those who use it are often masters of the airwaves. They have skills at shifting dimensions and getting "downloads." In everyday life (the third dimension), she may not be as effective as other pattern types. But in the dimensions where she goes when she leaves her body, she is quite masterful and may even have various forms of extrasensory perception.

The key to navigating out of this pattern is to claim the right to exist, claim the space inside her field and inside her core entirely for herself, and not let anything push her out of her body again.

The Oral Pattern

The oral pattern is born of an attempt to settle one's nervous system using connections with others. If a person runs this pattern, they will seek out others consciously or unconsciously to try to feel better.

The oral pattern manifests in two ways: full oral and compensated oral. I have met very few people who use the oral pattern who do not also have the compensator. The straight oral pattern tends to cause a kind of energetic "puddling" that is often expressed as self-pity. It is as though the neediness is too much to hold, and the person collapses in on themselves and looks for someone to rescue them. Some people who run the oral patterns find themselves repulsed by their own neediness. The straight oral pattern is just too hard to accept, so the compensator comes online. The compensator rejects the victim mentality by using all the other energy patterns to avoid falling apart or puddling. She will pretend that she is fine and has her ducks in a row, even though it's not true. Generally, when a compensator appears upset but says she is fine, she is definitely *not* fine. Sometimes she will say, "I'm fine," as a cover to hide her pain. Other times it's because she has hidden her pain from herself. This pattern developed as a means for survival in the first few years of life. She may have been denied the care and nurturing that she needed during that particular stage of development.

For example, if food was scarce and her mother could not breastfeed her, she was always hungry. That feeling of a hollow core became habitualized. The craving for satisfaction and fullness that were never fulfilled manifested in this sense of inadequacy and helplessness. This pattern prevents her from experiencing the authentic present, as she gets trapped by the unmet needs she experienced during her early development. Consequently, she sees through the lens of scarcity, creating the energy of neediness and fragility. If she is in the oral pattern, she will likely be extremely clingy and will crave attention. Or, if she runs the compensated oral pattern, she will go to heroic lengths to hide her neediness from herself and others. The compensated oral pattern is a mask that many who have the oral pattern will wear to pretend that everything is alright when it clearly is not. She rejects her needs and projects them onto others. Then, rather than focusing on her own needs, she focuses on the real or projected needs of others.

The compensation is only a mask covering the unfinished work of this stage of development. So, the compensated oral has two rounds of work: to remove the mask and then address the neediness. On the other hand, the oral is deeply aware of her neediness, as are those in her life. In both situations, she practices referencing others and avoids referencing herself. The healing comes when she can make friends with her neediness and learn how to skillfully ask for what she wants and needs before the discomfort becomes so strong that she puddles or compensates.

The gift of this strategy is that by being so tuned in to others, she becomes skillful at sensing their needs and providing what's needed. In this way, people with this pattern can be extremely thoughtful and caring, often excellent at predicting needs. However, those with oral pattern (both types) run the risk of training their partners to expect having their needs met first. If compensated, they may also successfully fool their partner into believing they don't have many needs. This can cause deep resentment as those who run oral often expect their partner will return their thoughtfulness and skill at meeting needs. This is the classic martyr/victim syndrome.

The Masochist Pattern

To understand this pattern, it helps to imagine our energy to be tree-like. Someone who uses this pattern is well-rooted into the earth, with their energy and attention largely focused below ground. She will take in information very slowly through her roots. If energy moves too quickly for her to receive the message, she will respond with an automatic "No" which is really just a form of "stop" or a request for more time to process. People who run the masochist pattern are typically more patient, so they are sometimes referred to as "endurers." However, this can become destructive as they may endure too long, past their breaking point. This pattern was likely created by an overbearing and controlling parent or caregiver who dominated or humiliated the child, creating an inner rebellion. On the outside, she may be passive, but on the inside, she is a ticking time bomb when ignited. She might withdraw internally and implode to avoid exploding or revealing her needs, desires, and emotions. She will be tolerant to the extreme until she can't take it anymore, then she will snap.

People who use this pattern feel very solid and grounded. They do not swing around wildly or appear over-energized. The gift of this pattern is the ability to provide that grounding earth element energy to both themselves and others. They are very helpful in group settings.

The key for people who run the masochist pattern is honing the ability to recognize where their boundaries are and effectively sharing that information with others *before* it becomes intolerable. Once they hit that point of becoming triggered, the communication will likely be harsh and unloving. For example, Anita was married for eighteen years. She was the sole provider in the relationship. Her husband was in a band and traveled around a lot. He was also polyamorous and chronically ill with an auto-immune disease. After one session that awakened Anita's sexual energy, she realized that she was done with the relationship and wanted a divorce. While her discontent had been under the surface for years, the decision to leave was quick and final.

The Psychopath Pattern

The psychopath pattern manifests as a "revving up" or a boost of energy and adrenaline to the system when triggered. This creates a win-lose dynamic, and the person is ready to pounce or blast their perceived opponent to make sure that they win. Like all patterns, this one is also designed to help people feel safe. But because it is so aggressive in nature, it can be difficult to imagine that those who use it feel scared.

This is my primary pattern. Because I was in my mother's womb when she was thrown down a flight of stairs, I was instantly armed with the psychopath pattern as a survival mechanism. I was born pumped with adrenaline, resulting in having very long arms and legs and a short body.

For those who faced dangers such as this, the pattern is a safe-haven of the utmost importance. A life-threatening situation occurred, and he was too little to defend himself. Because nobody came to his rescue, he wills himself to get through the terror without any support from the people who should have been there. This also manifests as difficulty trusting other people. He creates safety by being an alpha and dominating or controlling situations and sometimes people.

The gift of this pattern is having a strong sense of self, personal power or will-power, and the ability to defend himself and his space or territory. People with this pattern are often seen as natural leaders because they are willing to take charge. Many politicians run this pattern. It's great in times of war, not so great times of peace (they don't really use diplomacy as a tactic) or when the enemy cannot be directly engaged or easily contained, as is the case with terrorist groups and pandemics.

The key to navigating this pattern for a person who runs a psychopath as a primary pattern is surrendering to something larger than themselves. They must find something that provides a sense of purpose, safety, and containment in a way that wasn't available in early childhood. For me, it is my mission. It is my purpose.

The Rigid Pattern

The rigid pattern manifests itself as a need to depend upon rules for structure, direction, and certainty. People who operate in this pattern have a strong drive for perfection and high performance. For someone who runs this pattern, when the energy is in overload and he gets triggered, the coping strategy is to surrender to outside rules. The rigid survival pattern is all about the need to be perfect and not make any mistakes to try to feel safe.

I know this pattern well because it is my secondary pattern. I can recall with great clarity that specific moment when I believe that I became armed with the rigid pattern. I was somewhere between four and five years old when my father told me to come outside and help him work on a car that was parked in the driveway. He was making some kind of repair to it and he wanted me to hold a flashlight so he could see what he was doing. We were both lying down under the car, me holding the flashlight, him trying to work. I had no shirt on. Because the cement was cold, I struggled to keep the flashlight still. He got so annoyed with me that he smacked me upside my head and hollered, "Hold the fucking flashlight still god-damn it!" Fearing for my safety, my ability to hold the flashlight perfectly still became instantaneously attainable and even easy for me. I used the rigid body-structure to avoid repeating my mistake and getting smacked again.

The gifts of the rigid pattern are organizational skills, overall competency, and the ability to pay attention and follow the rules. To successfully navigate out of this pattern and into Presence, fill your belly with breath and light while gently opening the heart. I have a mantra that helps me soften this pattern: "I will not judge; I will witness and experience the present moment."

You Are Not Your Pattern

It is important to understand that people are not their patterns. The patterns, much like old stories or programming from child-hood, can pull people from the present moment back to the past energetic response that saved them in an extreme situation. We all have patterns that can be activated when we are unable to hold the energy that has been generated as a response to the reality of the moment. Catching yourself when you are in pattern, or ideally just before you go into pattern, then shifting back to Presence is the goal. To learn more about this critical work, you can read *The 5 Personality Patterns: Your Guide to Understanding Yourself and Others and Developing Emotional Maturity* by Steven Kessler, perhaps the most complete and accessible book on the topic.

Learning to master your energy before you get overloaded is essential to living a happy and productive life. But you don't have to just roll the dice on this. As a Soldier of Love, you will need to lead the way when it comes to mastering your energy and your energy patterns. To help you with that, you can use The Energetic Essentials, a set of practices that work for all the energy patterns.

The Energetic Essentials

The Essentials are derived from a combination of tools and techniques from several art forms, including but not limited to martial arts, qi gong, tantra, and Taoism combined with indigenous energy tools. Together they form a potent practice that prepares you to run energy safely and effectively. This practice is also the best way to embody Presence, which is the antidote to being triggered or put in pattern. In a nutshell, the Essentials are a way of stepping into your power with clarity and balance.

I have created the following guided meditation to enable you to move through the practice of bringing your Essentials online easily.

A free audio version of this meditation, along with the workbook is available at **SoldierofLoveWorkbook.com**. Practicing this guided meditation daily cultivates your capacity to stay present. Bringing your attention and intention to the meditation will strengthen and deepen your ability to be present more often, regardless of what's happening around you. As you do the visualizations and breathing exercises, you will move into a peak state in which you can create new patterns of thought.

The breathing modality needed to get the most from this practice is called *connected breathing.* In connected breathing, every inhalation is connected to the exhalation, allowing the energy to continuously move without pause.

I activate my Essentials before every coaching or energy work session, before stepping out onto the stage to teach or speak, or before moving into a crowded room where the energy may get chaotic or distracting. It is non-negotiable for me, and I highly recommend it. I have written the steps here. You may wish to record them into your phone and play them back (or you can access a free audio recording of this exercise at **SoldierofLoveWorkbook.com.**

Step 1: Get Centered

You will focus on the center of your body (your core) and visualize glowing energy in and around your spinal cord.

Allow the core of your body to fill up with light so that your spinal cord, your central nervous system, and all the muscles around them begin to glow. Let the glow grow until it fills you up, reaching to the inside edge of your skin. Imagine holding your arms out as though you are going to fly. Your fingertips will be touching the edge of your body's auric field. Your field is an egg-shaped bubble, and you want to be directly in the middle of it. Make whatever adjustments are needed to center yourself in your field. Once you are centered in your body and centered in your field, you're ready to get grounded.

Step 2: Get Grounded

You will focus on your feet and tailbone while visualizing the energy roots of your body growing into the earth.

Visualize the glow in your body increasing in size and density. See and feel the glow begin to grow out of your toes, your feet, and the base of your spine, creating tree-like roots that penetrate the earth. See and feel the roots reach all the way down to the center of the earth, connecting with every root of every tree, bush, plant, and flower on the way down. Once the roots touch the center of the earth, see and feel them wrap around the magma core like two giant hands holding a baby apple.

Step 3: Energize Your Body

You will visualize bringing energy from the earth's core and the sun into your body.

Now that you are centered and grounded, see and feel your connection with the earth increasing in power, enhancing your sensations of connection. Notice how your roots are impervious to heat, as they begin to magnetize and sip the life force energy from the center of the earth up through the roots and into your core. With each breath, continue sipping up the earth's energy into your body through your roots.

Now turn your attention upward by visualizing all the sunlight filtering down through the atmosphere onto the planet. Notice that there is a single special ray that is uniquely available just to you. See and feel yourself connecting to your own unique sun's ray by visualizing the ray coming down into your field. See and feel it entering your body through the back of your brain and the top of your spine in the back of your neck. Allow the core of your body to magnetize life force energy from the center of the earth below and the energy of the sun above meeting in your center. These energies keep you invigorated and energized.

Step 4: Seal Your Edges

You will visualize and strengthen the edge of your auric field.

Now visualize your egg-shaped energy field surrounding your body. By now, it will be glowing more brightly. Bring your attention to the edge of your field. Notice it has a membrane along that edge all the way around it. Visualize the edge of your field being crisp and clean and free from any pores, nooks, crannies, cracks, or holes. Breathe energy into your edge and empower it to be stronger. Allow it to template the earth's edge, which is so strong that it burns up or bounces off billions of pieces of space junk. Notice how your edge is now able to burn up or bounce off junk energy that comes your way, keeping your bubble clear.

Step 5: Tie Your Fibers

You will locate and tie the energetic fibers that reach outward from your core.

Like all cells, we have structures that look like fibers that stretch out from our bodies to interact with the world around us. Two of these fibers are quite long. They come from our belly, similar to the umbilical cord we had in the womb; however, these are designed for feeling. If we are walking around in the dark, climbing trees, mountains, or hills, our fibers come in quite handy. However, if we are not using our fibers for climbing and moving around the dark, they can often hinder connections and be harmful and destructive.

Allow yourself to become aware of and visualize your main fibers moving outward from your belly. Imagine holding one in each of your hands. Gently bring each fiber around to the back of your body. Insert your fibers into your back and imagine pulling them through your body and coming out of the front of your belly, like shoelaces. Visualize wrapping the remaining part around your body twice. Now tie them off just like you would a martial arts belt, looping one side around the other and quickly pull the left hand up and right hand down into a knot.

Get the Audio

Visit **SoldierofLoveWorkbook.com** for a free audio version of this meditation. It will walk you through the steps so you can follow my voice instead of thinking or reading. You will get centered, grounded, and connected to the earth, and the sun's life force energy to energize yourself and connect with your unique sun's ray. You will shore up and empower your edge and tie your fibers securely. With that, all your Energetic Essentials will be active.

Working with the Energy of the Earth

Most people tend to feel happier and more peaceful when they're out enjoying nature. This is partly because of the absence of man-made vibrations. Without interference from the electromagnetic frequencies from radios, televisions, computers, city lights, and the noise created by trains, planes, and automobiles, the human body can align itself with the healing vibration of Mother Earth's coherent field.

Without these distractions, it is much easier to connect to the earth's grounding energy and the calming natural frequency of the planet itself. Earth is like an enormous electric circuit generating an electromagnetic field that surrounds and protects all living things. When tuned into the Earth's natural frequency, the human body can benefit greatly by becoming energized and revitalized, promoting healing and restoration. This healing frequency pulsates at 7.83 hertz (cycles per second). This pulsation is likened to the Earth's heartbeat. The human brain's average alpha frequency in electroencephalography is also 7.83 hertz.

The magnetic field surrounding the earth is radiated from heat from its molten core of iron and nickel (Fe) and (Ni) 10,800 degrees Fahrenheit or 6,000 degrees Celsius, enabling the earth to give off life force energy. This means that even without the heat of the sun (where most of our energy comes from), the earth would be warmer than space and any planet without a molten core. Energy is a property that cannot be created or destroyed; however, it can be influenced to change, move, or be transferred and transformed. Electromagnetic fields are dynamic entities that impact other charges and currents to move and are also influenced by them.

The important thing to remember is that the life force energy of the earth can be harnessed and transferred so that it positively affects the human experience in several palpable ways. By plugging into the earth's energy and tuning into its frequency, we can live longer and better lives. Tune into the Earth's heartbeat and allow it to nourish you like a mother nursing a newborn baby. The following exercise is a visual that can help you with this.

Building Your Blueprint Exercise: Connect with the Earth

Find a place on the earth; perhaps it will be your front or back lawn, ideally where trees surround you. If you can get away from the city noise and as many distractions as possible, even better. Tune in to the Earth's coherent field. You will be able to template, or "copy" this field, allowing your field to become coherent. You will also be able to reach for energy from the Earth to use to rejuvenate, revitalize, and energize your body. While tuning into the Earth's unique frequency, breathe deeply and slowly. Visualize yourself storing this energy in your bones and tissues. (To make this easier, you can access a free audio version of this meditation and the workbook at **SoldierofLoveWorkbook.com**.)

Remember, energy is your most precious commodity, more valuable than time or money. Now that you have a good foundation for how you will master your energy, it's important to consider how to keep your energy flowing well. The best way to protect and conserve your energy is to live and work from a place of balance. The next chapter explores this vital topic.

"Happiness is not a matter of intensity but of balance and order and rhythm and harmony."

—Thomas Merton

"The best and safest thing is to keep a balance in your life, acknowledge the great powers around us and in us. If you can do that, and live that way, you are really a wise man."

—Euripides

Chapter 5

LIVING IN BALANCE

A recent study by the National Safety Council (NSC) found that 97 percent of Americans say that they have at least one of the leading risk factors for fatigue, including anxiety, stressful work environments, poor sleep habits, poor eating habits, long commutes, overworking, working nights, chaotic social situations, and toxic politics. According to a 2017 survey by the NSC, nearly half of all Americans are too sleep-deprived to mitigate critical risks that can jeopardize safety at work and on the road, including the lack of ability to focus, think clearly, make informed decisions, and be productive. About 76 percent of Americans say they feel tired at work, and 44 percent admit that they struggle to focus.

According to the NSC, fatigue has reached epidemic proportions, impacting most Americans and causing disastrous outcomes all too often. Think about this: A person who has lost two hours of sleep in an 8-hour night is as impaired as if they had consumed three beers. Imagine how you would feel knowing your child's teacher came to work after a breakfast of three beers? What about your Uber or Lyft driver? Or your boss? Fatigue and low-energy is a huge barrier to our evolution as individuals and as a people. Most of us are so tired that we barely make it through the day before falling back into bed a night. No wonder we stay stuck! In that state, who has the time or energy to evolve?

These findings are a literal wake-up call. Stress and other diseases can cause imbalances in your body, manifesting as chronic pain, anxiety, fatigue, and terminal illness. On the other hand, when you live in a balanced way, you have an abundance of energy. You feel creative, ambitious, empowered, motivated, clear, focused, upbeat, and productive. When you have enough energy, life is good. You feel more loving, healthier, happier, kinder, more intelligent, and even luckier. You are more pleasant to be around. With the proper amount of energy, the delicate systems in your body can function optimally. Your digestive system, your nervous system, your immune system, your endocrine system, and your pleasure and pain systems all work best when you live in balance.

As a Soldier of Love, you need to be committed to the work for the long haul. To make good on that commitment, I cannot emphasize enough the importance of living in balance. Balance is the key to flow and functionality. I dare to say that it may be the most important of all of the lessons that I share.

Those of us who are dedicated to service and healing work may be at greater risk of living out of balance because we know what is at stake. We are passionate about helping others and about healing the planet. But we simply cannot serve beyond what is healthy, or we become a danger to ourselves and others. Some of my learning around the critical need for balance came the hard way.

The Risks of Light-Working

The usual definition of a lightworker is somebody who works with other people to bring more light into their life and into their world. This can look many different ways. For example, a massage therapist can be a lightworker, assuming they have good intentions and infuse their work with healing energy. Doctors, hypnotherapists, acupuncturists, chiropractors, psychotherapists, and therapists of all kinds who have good intentions are also lightworkers by this definition.

However, a lightworker who is not in balance is actually a light-slave. I experienced a major shift when I first learned of the critical difference between operating as a lightworker and a light-slave. For nearly two decades, I had operated under the illusion that my mission itself was my spouse. People would ask me questions like, "Will you ever get married again?" Or, "Will you ever find one woman and spend the rest of your life with her?" My typical answer was, "No. I already have a beloved, and that is my mission."

I believed that having a wife or a serious girlfriend would be a distraction. I believed that having a spouse who would need, desire, and deserve my time and attention would take away from my mission. I made casual connections and had loving relationships to a certain degree, but I refused to commit. I was always committed to making my lovers happy while we were together and satisfying her in and out of the bedroom to the best of my ability. But she could only get so far with me as a partner because I didn't believe that I had the room to succeed in my mission and be in a committed relationship. This illusion got shattered in a single moment on my first sacred journey to Egypt.

While in Egypt, the group that I was co-leading had a private workshop with a powerful teacher named Gamal. Gamal is an incredible man who has no website, no internet, and no need or desire to advertise his offerings. He is a true master of his craft. His ability to see me clearly, even though he had just met me a few moments before, was mind-blowing. I now consider Gamal one of my great teachers.

During that first visit, Gamal told me things about myself that opened my eyes in a way they had never been opened before. That day I learned that I was not functioning as a lightworker; instead,

I was a light-slave. He told me with great intensity that I need to cultivate a healthy, active, and fulfilling personal life. At first, his words were hard to take in. This idea of a light-slave was a foreign concept to me.

Furthermore, I thought that I did have a compelling personal life. But in truth, I did not. When I reflected honestly, I could see that all the things I wished for my clients I was withholding from myself. Gamal shared with me the changes that I could make to free myself from operating as a light-slave, and I committed to change my ways.

Making these changes brought more balance in my life, allowing me to enjoy relationships in a way that I hadn't in years—not since I had started doing Tantric work. I am happy to say that I now have the active and fulfilling personal life that Gamal recommended while still remaining in alignment in my professional life. This is one of the greatest gifts that I have ever received.

The Wounded Healer

Another way of thinking about the term light-slave is to look at it through the lens of the Wounded Healer Archetype. I know many wounded healers—men and women who have uncanny skills but simply do not take good care of their bodies. I know people who have unique and highly sought after offerings who seem unable to balance their checkbook. I have met people who work out four hours a day and eat an incredibly healthy diet who never stretch, so they continuously pull muscles. I have met people who exercise, have a healthy diet, do yoga, and have dedicated themselves to being healthy, except they have incredibly poor sleeping habits. Then they wonder why they get ill. You may know many of these people too. You may even be one—like I was.

But no matter what the specific goal is for your service work or mission in the world, to attain it at the highest level that you are capable of, you must be at your best. That means you must have cultivated a lifestyle that honors the imperative of living in balance. Having good intentions is not enough. We must have a plan that maximizes our ability to be effective and make an impact in the world. My philosophy is that we need to consciously focus our energy and make constant micro-adjustments to be balanced energetically, emotionally, physically, spiritually, professionally, and financially.

To be the highest functioning version of yourself, you must balance your personal life and professional life. Our bodies are incredible machines when we are in balance. When we are not in balance, we tend to get ill. To be healthy, you must be able to balance diet, exercise, and rest.

When I was growing up, the importance of staying hydrated was seldom understood. We drank Dr. Pepper and Coca-Cola rather than water at track meets, basketball games, football games, and other sporting activities. I worked out hard, and I stretched a lot. But I didn't drink enough water, and I had poor sleep habits, so I always had muscle spasms. I had debilitating spasms in my hamstrings and calves more times than I can count. The spasms probably never would have appeared had I known how vital hydration and sleep were. I would have made sure to drink water and sleep to protect myself and perform at high levels for long periods in the most healthy way possible.

It is now common knowledge that we must stay hydrated and drink an appropriate amount of water every day no matter what. It is becoming better understood that the amount and quality of our sleep can determine how much energy and strength we can enjoy in our lives. I also believe that more people understand the need to stretch and exercise their muscles. However, most people do not understand that our subconscious programming and the energetic habits of attention we have formed during childhood can be equally as dangerous as ignoring our basic physical needs. These old, outdated programs can create massive imbalance in our bodies and our lives.

When I was young, I lived mostly in impoverished areas. The first time I left California was my junior year in high school when some friends and I drove to Lake Tahoe—just across Nevada's state line. I left the state a few more times for track meets, but I never did any real traveling until I was twenty-one when I spent a summer in Sweden. I learned more about life that summer than any other summer before (more about that in Chapter 7).

My experience in Sweden instilled in me a life-long love of travel. For the past three decades, I have gone all over the globe. My favorite places include Hawaii, Thailand, Egypt, and Costa Rica. By now, I have traveled so much that staying home seems like more fun than anywhere that I could go. This comes in incredibly handy in a fast-paced world where burnout is the norm. Staying home has become a national pastime in our new CoVid-19 world. Yet, some people feel stressed out because they need to stay home and cut back on travel. For me, it's a blessing not having to travel so much. There were times that I traveled so much that being in balance became incredibly challenging. It's challenging to eat healthy food when you're spending so much time in airports and on airplanes. It's difficult to get enough sleep when you're constantly crossing time zones or changing from airplanes to hotels to AirBNBs to retreat centers and back home. Because traveling and working with clients can be fun, the imbalance can creep up on us if we aren't careful.

Living in balance feels great. If your energy is balanced and your life is in balance, you will feel phenomenal. When you are out of balance, you will feel unwell. This sort of imbalance can be a result of diet, sleep, exercise, or energetic hygiene. Imbalance can also come from where you regularly place your attention: how much you give and receive love and nurturing, how much you put out, and how much you take in. That doesn't mean you won't occasionally lose it. We all do. But when our lives are fundamentally balanced, we can recover ourselves quickly and shift back into the energy of love.

Being fully present and measuring with your core will help you know when you are out of balance. If you listen, your body will let you know—dysfunction or disease may manifest, or even just simple aches and pains. If you listen to the smallest whispers, you will be able to course-correct before things go too far. This may take some practice to master. Again, I emphasize that to manage anything effectively, you must be able to measure it effectively.

Measuring Our State of Being

One way to ensure that we stay in balance is to manage all of the events in our lives effectively. To manage anything effectively, we must be able to measure it. This means answering questions like:

- How much time do I want to spend at home, and how much time do I want to spend traveling?
- How much time should I spend in the gym or working out at home?
- How much time should I spend on the yoga mat?
- What time should I go to sleep?
- What things can I do to ensure that my sleep is deep, restful, and rejuvenating?

- What kind of foods should I eat, and how much of them should I eat? And perhaps most importantly...
- How should I interact with and honor my most precious resource, my energy?

Where you put your time and energy is vital. Who you spend your time with and how they affect you is another crucial aspect that needs to be measured. If you surround yourself with people who are easily angered, who complain a lot, and who drain your energy, you will likely have a hard time remaining in balance. This is definitely true for me. As I have grown wiser and more committed to staying in balance, I have become very selective about who I surround myself with and who I offer my time and energy to, personally and professionally.

By creating a way of measuring all the aspects of your life that need to be balanced, you can better manage your energy, time, and choices. With practice, you will be more effective, efficient, productive, and the highest functioning version of yourself possible.

Things to Measure:

- Fatigue vs. enthusiasm
- Clear eyes, clear skin, clear tongue
- Aches and pains vs. moving with ease
- Number and intensity of arguments with your beloved
- Time with friends vs. time at work
- Numbing behaviors such as overeating, drinking, watching TV, scrolling on social media, and recreational drug use
- Judgment and irritation vs. a sense of generosity and forgiveness
- Time in spiritual practice
- Time exercising, resting and enjoying nature
- Amount of water and healthy food you intake

- Passion for life and satisfaction with work and play
- Clean and organized living space
- Loving connections with friends and family

Building Your Blueprint Exercise: Taking Stock Part 1

Rate the areas in your life to see which may need more attention. This accounting should consider the mental, physical, spiritual, emotional, sexual, financial, social, and professional areas of your life. Rate each one from 1 to 10 in how much satisfaction your experience in each area: 1 being the lowest and 10 being the highest. Then ask your body if any areas would benefit from less or more of your intention.

Boundaries With Others

One of the fastest ways we get out of balance is by not setting and maintaining good boundaries with the people in our lives. Having healthy physical, energetic, and emotional boundaries is crucial to minimizing misunderstandings and maximizing and maintaining a healthy level of safety in relationship to yourself and others. Physical and emotional discomfort in personal and social situations can often be symptomatic of having poor boundaries (for example, if you are somebody who hates being hugged yet frequently goes to places where everybody hugs you.)

The internalized discomfort could easily be avoided by simply stating your preference. In the CoVid-19 world, it's not such a challenge to be a non-hugger. But we will eventually be back in groups once more. We don't always want to hug everyone or even anyone. If your physical boundaries were not respected as a child, you might not know how to claim your space. But you have the right to choose where and when and with whom you have physical contact. The technique that I use when seeking to avoid a hug is to bring my hands to my chest and bow in the *Namaste* greeting. It still shows people you care but helps you avoid unwanted contact. If you always feel that people are trespassing against you, perhaps you have not effectively articulated your boundaries. Having lots of social regrets around how you allowed people to treat you is also the sign that they probably have not effectively acknowledged and articulated your boundaries.

Having healthy physical boundaries means honoring the space around yourself and the space around every other person. This means carefully considering how we approach someone, when and how to touch them, and when to give them more space. It is crucial to effectively express and understand your boundaries and the boundaries of those around you in order to honor them. Sometimes people in the spiritual healing world don't give a lot of attention to boundaries. Others seem to think that in romantic relationships, specifically in sexual union, boundaries impede achieving higher states of consciousness. However, boundaries are essential for creating the kind of safety needed for surrender and union to occur.

For the sixteen or so years that I was doing hands-on sexual activation sessions, most of my clients would say that they did not want to have boundaries in our session work. Many would express that they came to me expressly to dissolve their boundaries. Some would quote the master Tantric teacher Osho and his teachings on the bliss beyond boundaries. Or refer to their belief that Tantric experiences are supposed to be two people dissolving all boundaries and becoming one.

Despite their feelings on the subject, about 95 percent of the time, I would go ahead and set rigid boundaries despite their requests and maintain those boundaries during my sessions. To help them understand why I made that choice, I would relate the story of a powerful study on boundaries.

In this study, they would observe schoolchildren in a playground. Using control groups, they were able to witness unconscious behaviors that were dictated by whether or not they had put solid boundaries in place for the children. When there was no boundary around the play area, the kids behaved in a way that was constricted and contracted. They would watch as the schoolchildren huddled around the slide and swing set and hung out in line to ride the hobby horses or merry-go-round. However, in the same scenario, if there was a small fence surrounding the property, the kids would unconsciously feel safer, and, rather than standing around in clusters, they began to run and frolic and climb trees. They would play tag, Marco Polo, and hide-and-go-seek. With a safe perimeter, they felt free to expand—the complete opposite reaction to having no fence in place.

However, the worst-case scenario for the children occurred if the boundary was only partially present, such as a fence with holes in it or a shrub barrier that could easily be climbed or walked through. The same children who were unconsciously afraid to venture out would get curious and cross through the boundaries, potentially endangering themselves. It was as though they were finding a secret door, and they wanted to walk through it.

These results were consistent with my own. When simple boundaries were in place, it would allow the women I worked with to surrender more deeply into their feminine, enhancing the experience and increasing the chance that their desire to become sexually awakened and activated would come true.

As a Soldier of Love, you will be supporting others in their becoming. Your clients may sometimes feel challenged by their work with you. It is important to pay attention to the practice of maintaining good boundaries, even when it seems they aren't necessary. In the long run, you and your clients will have better results.

When we talk about being balanced, we refer to two things: inner balance and outer balance. Inner balance means your biochemical state; your moods, thoughts, and behaviors come from a place of balance. Much of this, we have already addressed in Cultivating Presence and Mastering Energy. Outer balance means accessing how much time and energy you put into different areas of your life, of what I call, categories of improvement. When you are looking at the categories of improvement, ask yourself these questions:

- How much time and energy are you putting into the things that feed you?
- How much time and energy are you spending on the things that serve your highest good?
- How much time and energy are you spending on things that truly make your life better?

A common conundrum I come up against when helping people achieve balance in life is the scarcity mentality, specifically around not having enough time. Often somebody will say they don't read more or go to the gym because they do not have time. However, when they do the exercises that I recommend, including creating the categories of improvement, and examining how they actually are using the time they have, they are often surprised to see all the time leaks that they never noticed before. Without realizing it, they have large chunks of time that they are losing by not being intentional. The process of accounting for their time has revealed that they may spend two or three hours a day on social media or watching television. That's somewhere between 10 to 15 hours per week that could be used more intentionally.

Sometimes a lack of outer balance will affect one's ability to achieve inner balance. This can look like being over-scheduled, or giving time and attention to media content that doesn't feed you. In today's polarized Facebook community, it can mean wasting time on senseless arguments. Or maybe it is simply numbing out as you scroll and scroll on Instagram or watch YouTube videos. These things can end up leaving you depleted and even on edge. For many people, not making time to move their bodies is a huge impediment to having inner balance. Exercise is a very effective way to increase your body's ability to produce feel-good hormones and off-load negative energy, saving you from hitting the circuit breaker moments we talked about in the previous chapter. If you are not making time for nurturing self-care activities, you may very well be jeopardizing your inner balance and your outer balance.

Building Your Blueprint Exercise: Taking Stock Part 2

In this exercise, you are going to set up a tracking document that will allow you to account for how you are investing your time daily. Just like with money, you need to know how much is coming in and how much is going out not to get over-drawn. To make this easier, you can download the free Soldier of Love Workbook from **SoldierofLoveWorkbook.com**. The workbook has sheets that are already designed to help you with these exercises.

Step 1: Set Up

Get seven clean sheets of paper and write each of the seven days of the week on a single sheet. So you will have one sheet with Monday on the top, the next with Tuesday, and so on.

Step 2: Fill In

Look at your schedule and write down all the activities you have planned for each of the next seven days on the corresponding sheet. It's also okay to batch items. So you could put "Work" for a three-hour time block before lunch without having to list all of the tasks you may do during that work block. Note down how much time you expect each item to take. Leave 2 to 4 lines of space between each item you have planned.

Step 3: Daily Adjustments

At night before going to sleep, take about 3 to 5 minutes to go over each sheet, paying attention to these three things:

- Review and adjust the times of the planned items. Sometimes an activity will take more or less time than we planned.
- If you planned something that didn't happen, scratch it out.
- Recall the things you did that day that were not planned and add them to the blank lines you left. Add in the amount of time each new activity took. It's okay to use the back of the sheet if the things you did overflow.

Step 4: Daily Accounting

After you have all the items from your day listed and the time you devoted to each item. Rate each item from 1 to 10 on how aligned they are with your higher good, with 1 being the lowest and 10 being the highest.

For example, suppose you are a television critic. In that case, it might be appropriate to spend two or three or even eight hours a day watching the specific television shows and rate that activity a 10 out of 10 because it brings in income. However, if you are an artist who paints portraits for a living and spend half of your day watching television, you may need to rate that activity a 2 or a 3 as not very aligned with your highest good. Anything that is part of your self-care should be listed as "SC" rather than a number.

Step 5: Analyzing

Once you have your list and every item is rated, take a good look at it and see if there are things that you rated as 1 to 4 that you can eliminate, delegate, or minimize in your day. Notice how many items (and how much time) you have listed as SC for self-care. Did you have too many or none at all? Strive to be more conscious as you move through the following day.

You don't have to do any of these steps perfectly. But do your best to capture the bulk of your time and how you are investing it. By the end of the week, you should see some changes in how you invest your time. Just by making the invisible measurable, you will be better positioned to make a conscious choice about your time. This will allow you to achieve inner balance and outer balance in your life and keep you from living as a light-slave or a wounded healer.

Now that we have examined the principles of living in balance, we want to integrate them into our lives. For that, we will need to focus on the next step to develop your Evolutionary Blueprint: Developing Discipline.

"A disciplined mind leads to happiness, and an undisciplined mind leads to suffering."

—His Holiness the Dalai Lama

"With self-discipline, most anything is possible."

—Theodore Roosevelt

Chapter 6

DEVELOPING DISCIPLINE

Becoming disciplined and developing the capacity to focus on what was needed in any moment was a matter of survival for me. One experience in particular stands out that happened when I was just four. It was a Saturday morning, which was my favorite part of the week. I lived for Saturday morning cartoons. Our tiny duplex had only two bedrooms. Our parents' bedroom had a crib in it for my infant sister Tracy, and I shared the other bedroom with my five older sisters. We had two sets of triple bunk beds, and I slept on the top of one.

That morning, my mother came in and told us that we had to clean the room immediately. My sisters were not very tidy. They had clothes lying all over the floor, their beds were not made, and they did not seem to care about my mother's request. I put my stuff away and made my bed. I came out of the room, thinking I would get to watch cartoons as my reward. However, my mother sent me back to the room to tell my sisters to clean up. They just ignored me. My sister Kim began to tease me—she could be quite mean sometimes. She climbed up on my bed and messed it up. So I climbed up and remade it, but she just messed it up again. When I tried to stop her, she threw me off of the top bunk. I hit the floor really hard, and she thought it was hilarious. My other sisters didn't step in to help me because "nobody messed with Kim." I tried to leave the room, but it was so small that she was able to keep her foot against the door so I couldn't get out. Eventually, my mother came back and got really angry that the room wasn't clean and the beds weren't made. I tried to explain the situation, but she didn't listen. Instead, she said that if it wasn't spotless in 10 minutes, we'd get our asses beat. I tried and failed to get my sisters to cooperate.

When our mother returned and saw that the room had not been cleaned, she pulled out a belt. Starting with my oldest sister, she bent her over and spanked her hard with the belt. I was terrified. Our mother worked her way down from Julie to Debbie to Kim to Tammy to Deanna, and then she came for me. But I fought to keep myself from getting spanked, which angered my mother even more. She pulled my pants down and spanked me with the belt on my bare bottom (I had welts on my butt for days.) After she was done, everybody got to go out and watch cartoons except me.

I felt angry, defeated, and hopeless. I found a pair of suspenders in the closet and tied them in a knot around my neck. Then I tied the other end onto the top of my bunk bed and jumped off, trying to hang myself. Fortunately, the suspenders snapped. I sat there thinking about how much I hated my life. I hated the neighborhood where I lived. I didn't like the way my sister was treating me. I did not like how my mother was treating me, and I was terrified of my father. I was thinking about other ways I could take my life when an apparition appeared to me. I saw a ten-foot-tall woman made of silver light shrink herself down to human size and float in the air in the lotus position. She blew in my ear and I heard the words, "I have a special mission for you." This changed everything for me. The impulse to end my life left me. It was replaced by a desire to figure out what she was talking about. It wasn't until thirty-three years later that I unraveled her mystery in the year 2000 at a Tony Robbins workshop (I'll share that story in Chapter 9.)

As you might imagine, in a house with constant chaos, I took solace and comfort in maintaining some small amount of control in my environment by having the discipline to keep my space neat. I became a complete neat freak. Later, when I was able to have my own room, it was always spotless. Even though I came by much of my discipline as a coping mechanism, it has been a great ally of mine over the years. Being disciplined helped me become a highly skilled athlete, an expert martial artist, a business owner, and a top-notch Daka.

Discipline is a quality that needs to be developed and practiced daily. There is a common misconception that being disciplined is something you are either born with or not. But, like other aspects of your personality, being disciplined is something that can be developed and mastered. What is the difference between the majority of people who would love to be healthier and happier and the minority who truly are? It is having the self-discipline following through on their desires and taking meaningful action.

Most people eventually develop the discipline that it takes to brush their teeth after every meal or at least once per day or twice a day. Fewer go the extra mile to floss daily. Most people eventually develop the discipline that it takes to maintain proper hygiene by taking showers, baths, and using specific products that allow them to appear and smell fresh. Fewer will keep their space neat and tidy. Many people have developed the discipline that it takes to get up and dress, commute to work, arrive on time and complete the daily tasks that it takes to maintain employment. Fewer will step out of their comfort zone to start a business or seek advancement.

As Soldiers of Love, we strive to be among the few, not just getting by with the minimum effort. To do that, I am challenging you to create even more healthy habits. The good news is you won't be starting from scratch. In fact, you are going to build on your successes. To do that, you will use the practice of "templating" the energetic fields of whatever habits you already have that are functioning well—those you may have developed out of necessity, as I did.

Building Your Blueprint: Using Lists

Develop the habit of making lists and checking off completed items, then transferring incomplete tasks to a new list for the following day. This may seem like a basic practice, but it is my observation that by simply making lists daily and paying attention to them, you start to develop more discipline to move your project forward.

Make a list, and you set your mind to accomplishing as many of the tasks every day as possible, paying particular attention to those that are the most important. Following through on this will give you the greatest boost. To give yourself a sense of real accomplishment, you can start by making a list of the things that you already do. As you feel the success of striking something off your list, you will come to enjoy being productive and eliminating tasks. You can make a list that starts with:

1. Wake up at 8 a.m.

2. Make breakfast

3. Wash and put away dishes

4. Take a shower

5. Feed the dog

6. Drive to work

7. Do a great job at work (maybe you have a separate work list you use from there)

8. Drive home

9. Connect with family

10. Make dinner

11. Wash and put away dishes

12. Watch a half-hour of television

13. Go to bed early

These are all things that require your time, attention, and energy. But we rarely give ourselves credit for all of these daily tasks that we are expected to do every single day. You should be able to check off most of these items each day. So you can add a few things, like making time in the morning and/or evening for self-care activities. In the same way you have learned to brush your teeth regularly, you can learn to do any daily practice. We start small with a 5-minute practice every day for seven days. The daily practice can be anything ranging from non-doing to guided meditations and exercise.

Make sure that you include 5 minutes of meditating, exercising, or doing something that qualifies as loving self-focus. As you progress in developing discipline, you will be able to elongate your practices. But in the beginning, keep it short and easy so that you have no excuse not to accomplish them. Eventually, it is ideal to work up to 20 to 40 minutes of a self-care ritual in the morning before work and another 20 to 40 minutes when you get home. That, combined with effective and healthy eating and sleeping habits, can completely transform your life. Discipline in our body and actions will be easier when we do the underlying work to be in integrity and alignment with our authentic self.

Energetic Integrity

A Soldier of Love needs to have integrity. Integrity, simply put, is a quality that keeps you in alignment with your most authentic desires and your inward and outward commitments. An excellent way to develop your integrity is the practice of doing what you say you're going to do. Keeping your word and living up to your commitments is crucial for developing a sense of trust with yourself and others.

For your energetic field to operate at maximum capacity, there must be alignment. But what are you aligning with? Many people have old wounds present within their field. That wounding keeps them stuck in patterns of perception, emotion, thoughts, and behavior. In one way, they believe they are acting in integrity because everything they see, feel, say, and do aligns with this inner wound. But the wounded self is not the authentic self, which means that they are actually aligned with something false.

True integrity is about aligning with your authentic self, which is why we continue to have painful experiences in life: to help us see and heal the wounding that is covering our authentic self-expression. While conflicts with others can hurt, they often serve to expose places where we are unconsciously trapped in our wounding and, therefore, not living our most authentic life.

For your field to operate optimally, you must be living in and aligning with your most authentic expression. It's an iterative process, and there is an effective body-based technique to help you become ever-more aligned with your authentic self.

Perhaps you've worked with a healer who uses the technique of muscle testing, which shows what strengthens or weakens your field. By posing a series of questions to your energy body through the physical body, you can access vast amounts of information. If you have not had one of these experiences, I strongly recommend going to San Diego and seeing Dr. Glenn Frieder, who uses muscle testing so precisely that he can give a specific antidote or homeopathic remedy. Freddy Ullan is a master teacher in the field of muscle testing, and his techniques are fascinating. Developing this skill is a simple yet powerful way of measuring when your field is in alignment. During an exercise at one of Freddy's workshops, one person holds her arm out and the other person tests by gently pushing down on the out-stretched arm while asking a series of questions. It doesn't take long before it becomes quite apparent when the person is telling the truth and when they are not. Their field gets stronger when speaking from the truth, and it's more difficult to push their arm down. When a person is lying or telling a partial truth, the energy in their field contracts and the field loses strength, making it much easier to push their arm down, even if they are consciously trying to resist.

When we are fully present, in alignment with our authentic self, and are practicing being in integrity, we are practically superhuman. When we are not in alignment, when we have no integrity, when we are dishonest with ourselves and others, even when we don't mean to be, our field weakens, manifesting itself in various forms of dysfunction, troubling thoughts, and illness.

Being Disciplined in Your Listening

Having perfect hearing is a blessing, but without proper listening skills, effective communication is unattainable. The sad truth is that listening is a skill that very few people ever master. Truly listening is more than just hearing the words that are offered. It also means being aware of how we can unintentionally distort the messages we receive.

One of the things that the human brain does most masterfully is to make up stories. Unfortunately, this blessing can also be a curse. And with us constantly looking at our phones, the average attention span is getting shorter and shorter. Most people only allow somebody to speak for a few moments before they cut them off. Maybe they were thinking of a story connected to the speaker's experience. Perhaps they are already formulating an answer or trying to predict what will come next. Or maybe they suddenly remember something they wanted to say earlier in the conversation and stop paying attention so they don't forget it. Whatever the reason, they aren't listening.

To truly listen, we must allow others to express themselves and complete their communications without judgment or any other block to listening. There are twelve blocks to listening to acknowledge and navigate so we can be disciplined in our listening.

Twelve Blocks to Listening

To be an active and effective listener, one must understand these blocks to listening and acquire the patience and attention span to listen skillfully. Without the awareness of these blocks and the skill to avoid them, it is challenging to have high-functioning communications. In today's deeply polarized landscape, the Soldier of Love must hold space and listen to differing points of view. Breaking the habit by using listening blocks is a must for creating the space needed to heal the division between people.

As you read the following list, be brutally honest about how often you engage with one of these listening blocks. Next to each item, mark N for never, S for sometimes and O for often.

1. **COMPARING:** Attempting to assess who is wiser, smarter, more competent, better educated, etc.

2. **MIND-READING:** Rather than genuinely paying attention to what people say, you are focused on trying to figure out what the other person is thinking, feeling, or about to say, often jumping to conclusions and finishing their sentences.

3. **REHEARSING:** Instead of genuinely listening, your attention is on preparing and crafting your next comment.

4. **FILTERING:** Paying just enough attention to see if there is a problem that requires attention, and once you determine it's safe to tune out, you allow your mind to wander.

5. **JUDGING:** Allowing critical thoughts about the other person to surface. Once you start judging them for any reason, it's quite challenging to be in the present moment enough to listen effectively—the more negative the judgment, the bigger the block.

6. **DREAMING:** A person says something that triggers a chain of thoughts for you. Memories and personal associations begin taking your attention away from the present moment into the past or future.

7. **IDENTIFYING:** Taking everything a person tells you and referring it back to your own experience. They tell you about an issue or experience that reminds you of an issue or experience that you have had, and your attention goes there, making effective listening almost impossible.

8. **ADVISING:** Rather than listening to the entire message being shared, you start prematurely problem-solving and offering solutions without having taken the time to fully understand what was being shared.

9. **SPARRING:** Quickly opposing and debating, never truly allowing the other person to feel heard.

10. **BEING RIGHT:** Going to any length to be right, including lying, exaggerating, twisting the facts, shouting, making excuses or accusations, calling up proof from the past, and avoiding being wrong.

11. **DERAILING:** By suddenly changing the subject, you derail the conversation as soon as you lose interest or become uncomfortable with the topic.

12. **PLACATING:** This is a form of people-pleasing. By prioritizing being likable and agreeable over really listening, you agree with everything without discernment.

Knowing these blocks is not enough to make you a competent listener. You must cultivate the skill of being an active listener. Active listening is when you allow somebody to complete their sentence or sentences and then repeat back to them what you heard them say, either exactly or paraphrasing. While it may seem cumbersome at first, this practice can eliminate a massive amount of misunderstandings. It will challenge you and help you see if you are listening.

Listening is a skill, and like all other skills it needs to be practiced and mastered. Becoming a great listener is one of the biggest gifts that you can give to yourself and others. For Soldiers of Love, it is an essential skill. If we have any hope of helping ourselves and our clients find common ground and evolve, we must first meet them where they are and listen with a fully engaged and compassionate heart.

Being Disciplined in Your Communications

Several years back, I was working with a couple who were struggling with their communication. I taught them about the importance of taking responsibility for the words they chose when communicating. This becomes very difficult when triggered. I taught them how important it is to take a break or a pause when they feel their energy rising. Otherwise, they will find it impossible to speak responsibly and carefully.

To practice personal responsibility, your actions, words, and feelings must be measured and shared from a place of deep honesty. You must have the discipline to be honest with yourself so that you can change and attune to your own feelings, wants, and needs, no matter what they may be. While this can feel risky or scary at times, it is essential for you to communicate clearly and with integrity in your relationship, and for your partner to better understand how you are feeling—a key component of every healthy relationship.

A strategy I like to use for implementing personal responsibility in how you present yourself is CLEAR communication, which stands for clear, loving, encouraging, authentic, and respectful.

Conscious Communication is about being responsible, mindful, and deliberate in speaking as well as listening. What you say and how you say it is of vital importance. Consider your words beforehand and understand what emotions they may evoke in the person you are speaking with. This is something few people do today, often resulting in prolonged circular arguments among couples and feelings of frustration that could have otherwise been avoided.

Effectively speaking consciously means being able to listen consciously as well. This is active listening vs. passive listening and requires paying attention to what your partner is saying in the moment rather than thinking about how you will respond. Our brains are often distracted or seek to validate our own perceptions, which can be easier said than done. If you notice you have drifted away from active listening, you can get back on track by admitting having drifted off and asking your partner to repeat themselves. Using the "mirror technique" is another way you can ensure your partner's voice is being heard. Repeat back to them what they have said to you and ask if you've heard correctly. This allows for clarification in the moment if needed.

Loving communication is not simply verbal affection but instead communicating with your partner from a place of love. The goal is connecting and sharing your love for one another effectively while sharing your perspectives, needs, desires, and requests in a way that works well for all involved. The opposite of this would be competitively speaking to each other, essentially keeping score and trying to prove that you are right. All this does is harm your relationship and create tension when arguments arise. This is when being right seems more important than being in harmony.

Encouraging communication is speaking in a way that is inspirational to your partner, encouraging them to be the best version of themselves they can be. This type of language builds relationships and creates a stronger bond between partners. A great example of how inspirational and encouraging language supports joint outcomes can be found in the metaphor of team sports. When teammates do well, we cheer. When they make a mistake, we call them up to remember their greatness and encourage them to stay in the game and try again. As a couple, you are playing together on the same team, not against each other. Speaking in a discouraging manner is a mutually detrimental practice that will only prevent your relationship from growing. Remind your partner just how valuable they are and how much they mean to you.

Authentic communication is just that: speaking truthfully and honestly. Hiding how you really feel and what you are thinking will only create unhealthy boundaries in your relationship. Tell your partner what you are looking for and how you feel while being mindful of your specific words and their possible impact. But take note, it can be easy to fall into the trap of communicating in a manipulative way, phrasing your words just to get what you want. Communicating authentically with kindness is the goal. Being kind and thoughtful is the opposite of manipulation. It is about wanting the communication to be successful and the connection to be strong, not necessarily about a particular outcome.

Respectful communication falls more in line with knowing what not to say and understanding when it should not be discussed, such as personal conversations in a public place, sore subjects, or referencing a past trauma that may evoke negative feelings. Be aware of your motives before bringing up something that might not be taken well. From a gender perspective, a man may try to control the conversation in a misogynistic way, speaking down to women, while a woman may attempt to emasculate men to gain the upper hand. Speak equally and with respect.

Now that you are clear about the importance of developing discipline and you have several keys for keeping your life and work flowing in a balanced way, it is time to create the kind of clarity you need to be sure that you are staying focused on the right things. The next chapter looks at how our old conditioning and programming gets in the way of our success and what you can do to shift yourself and clear your perceptions.

"It's a lack of clarity that creates chaos and frustration. Those emotions are poison to any living goal."

—Steve Maraboli

"When people will not weed their own minds, they are apt to be overrun by nettles."

—Horace Walpole

Chapter 7

CREATING CLARITY

Imagine that when you were born, you had a pair of glasses on that were perfectly clear. Imagine you wore these glasses everywhere until eventually, you didn't even notice that they were there anymore. Since you didn't notice that they were there, you never developed the habit of cleaning the lenses. And, as time passed, your lenses got more and more smudges, fingerprints, and smears. But it happens slowly, so you get used to looking at things through these smeared and smudged lenses. As a result, you see what I call the funhouse mirror effect. You know the mirror I am talking about; it warps your reflection to look taller, thinner, shorter, and wider than you really are. Like those mirrors, your dirty lenses are distorting your view. Even though you're looking at something with both eyes wide open, these dirty lenses keep you from seeing the reality of what you are viewing. The unfortunate part is that you will believe the things that you see with these faulty lenses.

You are not alone in this. Most people see life through this skewed and inaccurate point of view. You have been looking through those lenses for your whole life, and it's all you know. It's easy to understand how you would believe with all your heart that what you are seeing is true when, in most cases, it's a distortion. If you're living with limiting beliefs and fear-based thoughts, you will see things through that particular distorted lens. All of us pick up limiting beliefs about ourselves and the world in childhood. That is unavoidable. What is not unavoidable is being stuck with them. But first we have to have a mechanism to make them visible, to tune into them and see what they are and how they have distorted our view so that we can make the changes necessary to clear away their influence.

Do you remember the kind of radios that had a dial for tuning into a radio station? As you turned the dial left and right, you would hear lots of static when you were between stations. But as you got closer to a station, the static would decrease, and the signal being broadcast became clearer until eventually, you're on the station that is broadcasting the music that you want to hear loudly and clearly. My favorite station growing up was KSFX, the San Jose funk station. My sisters mostly listened to KLIV, which was more of a pop station. Either way, to find the frequency that played the specific music to our desire, we had to tune in to that exact station.

Human beings all have their own unique frequency and vibration. Like radio stations, we need to tune into our unique frequency to experience the truest and clearest version of ourselves. This can only be done when we are paying attention and noticing the static that is an indication that we aren't quite in tune.

Some principles and practices can help us remove the static so that we can find our own uniqueness. Using these practices to tune into the frequency of our unique vibration helps us see ourselves better. That, in turn, enables us to notice how clean or dirty our lenses are so that we can take the action needed to get a clearer view of what is outside of us. It may be shocking at first to so clearly see who you are and what you are looking at.

Building Your Blueprint Exercise: Unique Essence Meditation

Everything in the universe is made up of energy vibrating at different frequencies. These frequencies determine form. The number of unique frequencies is mind-boggling because every living being, including the things that don't appear to be living, has a unique frequency. The more alive something is, the more life force energy it has, and the more its frequency is transmitted beyond itself. Trees, plants, flowers, dogs, cats, birds, caterpillars, lions, and every human being have their unique vibration and essence.

You can imagine your essence is transmitted much like the signal of a radio station sends out. That signal is a transmission of whatever music they are broadcasting at the time. We, too, send out a transmission of whatever is going on for us in that moment. If we are vibrating in love, we send out the signal or vibration of love. If we are vibrating in fear, we send out a signal of fear. The more we are tuned in to our unique essence, the stronger that signal is. The same way that if you're not quite tuned in to the proper radio station, you might get static funds or other types of interference. When you tune in to your unique essence, you are your most authentic self. In all of history, past and future, there will never be an exact duplicate of you. Once you have truly tuned in to your unique essence, your signal will be more powerful and you will be able to receive other signals more clearly. This meditation is most effective if you have already done the Essentials meditation. I recommend doing this meditation when you don't have anything that has to be accomplished afterward, preferably when you have at least an hour to stay in a relaxed state.

The meditation works best if you sit in a chair with an erect spine and both feet planted firmly on the ground. Having an upright spine is like having a straight antenna in your inner spinal channel (flute) that allows energy to move up and down your body. Take care that your spine is not kinked and your head is not leaning to one side or the other, or the energy won't flow well—kind of like trying to water your lawn with a kink in your water hose. To open everything up, have your spine straight and take deep breaths while visualizing opening up your inner flute completely. Once your spine is open, you will tune in to the spark of light that holds all the energy, frequency, and information specific to you that has been collected over this lifetime and perhaps many others if you believe in such a thing. This spark of light is similar to a flash drive or tiny microchip that holds massive amounts of information.

You can read a description of the meditation below or download a free audio of this meditation at **SoldierofLoveWorkbook.com.**

Meditation Description

Begin by tuning into this spark of light that holds your unique essence. Next, bring your arms up from your sides to above your head as if you're hugging the sky. Then you will "catch" this spark of light between your finger tips or between your palms. Then slowly pull it down into your body, into your brain, through your crown chakra into your forehead and your third eye chakra, then down to your throat, heart, chest, belly, and then down into your genitals.

Then you return to the top of your head and use your hands to gently caress down from your brain over your face down your throat, your chest, your belly, and your genitals. Do this for 3 to 5 minutes—or longer if you're enjoying it. It's important that you're smiling while relaxing your face but still allowing your mouth to form a big authentic smile. Finally, push on the tops of your feet as though you are anchoring in your unique frequency. After that, find a place to lie down and continue breathing deeply and smiling brightly.

Doing this meditation will help you clarify your frequency. This will have the effect of shifting your vibration into one that is more deeply aligned with your unique frequency. For this reason, it's a good practice to imagine "sending" your new signal out to the people in your life that you want to be able to "find" you at the new vibrational location of your "station," as it might be slightly different. Similar to when you get a new email address, people can't find you if they don't spell it exactly right. This is also true when you have changed your vibrational frequency, so send out a signal immediately after doing the meditation with the vibration of love and smiling energy, letting everybody you desire to stay connected with know that this is where you are now.

You will need to revisit this exercise often to begin to develop a relationship with your unique essence until it becomes integrated within you. This activity builds on the practice of self-referencing, which we discussed in detail in Chapter 4, Mastering Energy. From a self-referenced place, you can clear your perceptions to see things as they are rather than through a distorted lens that hinders perception.

Now that you have tuned into your essence, cleared your lenses, and are better able to see who you really are, you can get clear about who you want to become. You can get clear about exactly what you want to bring into your life. You can get clear on what you want to do for a living, who you want to surround yourself with, and how you want to behave. Without clarity, you are moving through life being overly influenced by the environment and your past programming.

Building Your Blueprint Exercise: Expand & Clarify

After you have completed the above meditation, have your blueprint journal and a pen handy. Next, close and open your eyes, and imagine they are open for the first time. Practice seeing with new eyes.

Notice the colors and shapes you see. Jot down a few things you see, noticing what seems new about your environment.

Look at your list of things you want to improve in your life (from Chapter 4). Notice how this list appears from this place of cleared perceptions. What changes or alterations might you want to make?

Review your list of habits for balance (from Chapter 5). Notice how this list appears from this place of cleared perceptions. What changes or alterations might you want to make?

Seeing Clearly and Releasing Judgment

Even though Soldiers of Love are always seeking to evolve, we also know how to love and accept ourselves just where we are. Part of seeing clearly means not being at war with *what is* while we are also moving toward *what can be*. It's a paradox. What doctor can be of any help if he resents or has contempt for her patient? Carl Jung says it best, "We cannot change anything unless we accept it. Condemnation does not liberate; it oppresses."

Radical acceptance is one of the most powerful tools in the Soldier of Love's toolbox. It is essential for you to learn how to be in harmony with nature and how to use nature as a support system. To do this, you will have to work on being in a place of non-judgment. This does not mean you pretend something isn't happening. It simply means that you acknowledge and accept the reality, as ugly as it may be, and then make decisions from a place of non-judgment. Judgment imposes right and wrong on situations that just are.

The people you react to most strongly, whether with love or hate, are projections of your inner world. What you most hate is what you most deny in yourself. What you most love is what you most wish for in yourself. Use the mirror of relationships to guide your evolution. The goal is total self-knowledge and mastery in keeping yourself tuned into your unique frequency and keeping your lenses clear.

If you see something has to change to address an imbalance, you will have the clarity to see a new way forward. You may choose to make significant changes to your life because now that you see clearly, you know they aren't working for you. Or you may see that you need to put in place new or better boundaries for yourself or others. But you do not have to descend into blame and hatred. Those will just steal away the precious energy you need to make the changes or set the boundaries quickly, cleanly, and from a place of love.

When you are in a place of judgment, you step out of the vibration of love and let go of the present moment. When you judge, you cut off understanding and shut down the potential for reconciliation. Hurt and disappointment are natural parts of all human relationships, including your relationship with yourself. If you are not in the habit of being loving and non-judgmental toward yourself, it will be impossible to extend that spirit of generosity to others. In judging others, you are showing yourself places where you may lack self-acceptance. Again, remember that non-judgment and self-acceptance don't mean you give up your capacity to discern. Loving yourself means you will use your cleared perceptions to get real about what is and isn't working for you. Non-judgment allows you to pivot away from that which isn't working with minimal disruption and emotional baggage.

Judgment and blame are symptoms of placing your power outside of yourself. It can be the difference between healing and moving on and staying stuck in old loops. You may need to forgive yourself for not seeing things sooner. You may need to forgive someone else for not living up to your expectations. You may need to forgive life for not being what you want it to be. Remember that each time you forgive, it adds to your capacity for self-love.

In high-functioning relationships, challenges are dealt with efficiently, effectively, and swiftly. Low-functioning relationships spend most of their time in conflict, anger, and disappointment.

The typical scenario in a conflict is spending 95 percent of the time and energy expressing the dislike over and over again, rather than seeing the reality and taking action to address it. Blame and judgment cause this loop. Whether you are unconsciously blaming yourself or consciously blaming the other, it doesn't matter. That vibration keeps people in defended states and keeps solutions from coming to the forefront. It's a form of dysfunction we tend to tolerate because we don't see any other way; our lenses have always shown us this distortion, so we think it's all there is.

A high-functioning relationship is driven by self-mastery, conscious communication, and healthy habits that you cultivate and practice daily. High-functioning relationships allow you to bring out the best in each other rather than the worst. Choose to surround yourself with people who are willing to learn and grow. People who are not interested in developing or learning will keep themselves and others stuck in low-functioning and dysfunctional relationships. When you achieve a certain degree of self-actualization, what you most want will be there, and what you most dislike will begin to disappear. You will be able to maintain the connection to your unique frequency, with a healthy and coherent field, even in the most stressful of times. This will inoculate you against other-referencing, keep you in your power, and nip any tendency toward dependency in the bud.

Seeing and Moving Past Your Conditioning

If you took Psychology 101 in college or even studied biology in high school, you were likely introduced to the idea of disambiguation, or classical conditioning. In 1904, Ivan Pavlov was given the Nobel Prize for his demonstration that our physiology (physical response) could be conditioned or manipulated by external influences. His famous experiments became known by the shorthand phrase "Pavlov's dogs." These early experiments laid the groundwork for what we now call *neuro associative conditioning.* This is the technical name for the dirty lenses we have been talking about.

Pavlov was able to show that intentional conditioning (smudging or dirtying our lenses) can take place that alters and habituates a living being's response to a particular stimulus to the point where the original stimulus is no longer needed. In the experiment, Pavlov gave his dogs a little bit of meat powder, and as soon as the dog would begin salivating, Pavlov would ring a bell. He repeated this several times. Eventually he was able to show that by simply ringing the bell, the dog would salivate. As the dog salivated several times while the bell was ringing, it had developed a neuro association between the sound of the bell and the meat powder, until eventually the bell was enough to bring on the salivation response. It became automatic and beyond the control of the dog.

This knowledge comes in handy when it comes to breaking unconscious associations that do not serve your highest good. We all have past conditioning, some severe from childhood trauma or physical or sexual abuse, which forms these types of associations. Unless these associations are addressed in a professional setting, they may color our experiences with others. This can be an obstacle in relationships. Negative associations can be hidden at first, especially when we fall in love and our bodies are flooded with the hormones needed to form attachments. Eventually, those hormones wear off, and negative associations can override the energy and emotion of love in the relationship.

One couple I worked with offered a very clear example of this. I'll call them Cindy and Mike. Cindy, a former Tantra client, reached out to me in fear of losing her husband and her relationship. She explained that as soon as she got pregnant, Mike seemed to be repelled by her and altogether lost interest in connecting sexually. Cindy said that even after their daughter's birth, they were still not connecting sexually and seemed to be growing distant. Now little things were starting to bother her about him, and she feared he was having similar thoughts.

By the end of my first interview with them, I could see that the issue was based on their neural associations. Cindy was a first-time mother who had a very traumatic experience while giving birth. She was uncomfortable and nervous much of the time with the baby. Mike was a big, strong, intelligent man. But he worked as a salesman in a tech company surrounded by "nerds" who seemed to think they were better than him. This set up a difficult dynamic when Mike got home from work and would try to reconnect with Cindy.

Cindy spent most of her day feeling incompetent and lacking confidence. Plus, she was physically exhausted and overwhelmed by the experience of being a new mother, something that is quite common for new moms. Mike would head home from work, thinking about the experiences that he had throughout the day, many of which were unpleasant. During his drive through traffic to get home, he would ruminate on his dissatisfaction at work. He was not tracking, or aware of, what was waiting for him when he got home to his nervous wife and small child, both of whom need his masculine presence and complete attention.

When Mike would walk through the door, he'd often find Cindy overwhelmed with a crying infant. Both he and Cindy were agitated before reconnecting. Both were looking for relief from the other and not getting it. Eventually, much like Pavlov's dogs, their disappointment at seeing each other and not getting the relief they wanted became like the bell. But instead of salivating, they developed an aversion to each other. The good news is that they caught this early enough that the pattern could be interrupted. I asked them to be very intentional about reconnecting to push past the old signals.

Cindy knew what time Mike came home. Her assignment was to put the baby down for a nap or have a babysitter at the house. Then she could turn her attention to herself. Her commitment was to shower, brush her teeth, and put on something in which she felt pretty—whatever she would normally do if she were going on a date with Mike. As for Mike, his assignment was to wait to enter his home and see his two beautiful goddesses until he was in a happy and jolly mood. I suggested he start listening to a comedy station or his favorite music or on the way home or even have a conversation with an upbeat and funny friend.

Cindy agreed to be ready to greet Mike eagerly and lovingly—she would imagine jumping into his big strong arms and planting a big juicy kiss on him, which she was happy and excited to do. Mike agreed not to open the door until he was excited to see Cindy and looked forward to greeting her with a loving embrace and a juicy kiss. Nothing else had to happen, just this intentional exchange. They both knew it was going to take some effort to pull it off. But like the great students that they are, Cindy and Mike diligently followed through. It didn't take long until they developed new, more positive neuro associations related to each other by being present and available to each other and clearing their perceptions.

Cindy and Mike went on to have another daughter and then a son—their dream family. Years later, they have the skills they need to make adjustments any time they don't feel connected. They are intentionally "falling" more in love with each other all the time. Cindy and Mike made this turn around by being in acceptance from a place of non-judgment. They saw they had a problem and they both wanted to change it. They avoided blame and judgment and instead focused on clearing their perceptions and removing the "smudges" of the negative neuro association they had unconsciously created. They then created a vision of where they wanted to go and committed to moving toward that new reality. It may have felt awkward and even forced at first, but eventually, it became their new reality.

Clearing the Way for a New Vision

The sum of our experiences is just a sliver of what's possible in a world of infinite possibilities. Most of us have no idea what else we could do or be other than the things we have within our immediate surroundings. This is why education is such an essential part of evolution. Whether it's formal education or training or apprenticing with a knowledgeable teacher or coach, it's vital to have experiences that show us a different view, to help us see the smudges of our life experience, and clear our perceptions so we can find a better way forward. Travel is also one of the most powerful ways to recognize our conditioning and be offered an opportunity to change our perspective.

The summer I spent in Sweden at the age of twenty-one transformed me in ways that I could never have anticipated. Other than a short trip to Mexico, that was my first time outside of the United States. The trip to Sweden was a gift from my friend Patrick Sjoberg, a celebrity in the high jump world. We met when I was on the track team at San Diego State University and he traveled to the United States to compete. I had set the record at my high school by jumping 6 feet 8 inches and setting the junior-college record at West Valley College by jumping 6 feet 10 inches in height. From there, I was recruited to San Diego State. When Patrick was in town, I had a broken foot, so I wasn't doing much jumping. Patrick was jumping an impressive 7 feet 6 inches. But he was exhausted. He needed a break from his rigorous schedule and the pressure of his coach and stepfather. Since I was out of commission with my broken foot, we spent two weeks floating around in my pool in San Diego surrounded by beautiful women. We were having such a great time that Patrick went home later than planned. The rest and recreation were just what he needed. At his next meet, he jumped 7 feet 10½ inches, breaking the world record.

When my foot was healed, Patrick invited me to come to Sweden and stay with him for the entire summer to hang out and train together. He bought me a ticket to fly from San Diego to London, and from London, I was to take a ship to Sweden. Unfortunately, when I arrived in London, I was told that there was a mistake in the printing of the documents and that the boat that I needed to catch was not leaving for two days. I was stuck in London with very little cash and no real experience traveling. I went to a travel agent at the airport and explained my situation. He told me that he could get me a flat for £22.5 per night. I pleaded with him to find something more affordable that was closer to the airport, but he emphatically explained that this was all that he could do for me. I had only $200 to last me the entire summer, and I just couldn't spend almost $70 on a room. I didn't know what else to do, so I reluctantly handed over my cash.

As I was walking away from the travel agent, a young Vietnamese man with a French accent caught wind of what was going on. He pulled me aside and explained that I was being hustled because I was American. He said I should be able to get a room for under £10 a night, and he explained that the place the guy was giving me was extremely far away from the airport, requiring me to take public transportation for half an hour to get there.

I wasn't sure who to believe. He asked me to stand by and watch as he spoke to the travel agent. He walked in and said, "I need your least expensive flat near to the airport." The agent immediately booked him a room for £9.5 per night. As you can imagine, I was furious. I confronted the agent, saying I knew he was trying to hustle me. I said that he would just refund my money, we would have no problem. He began yelling at me, telling me I had to leave. The next thing I knew, I reached over the counter, grabbed him by his shirt, pulled him over the counter and into a chokehold, and told him to go back behind the counter and give me back my money.

Thankfully, he did, or I probably would have wound up in an English prison!

The whole experience was shocking to me. It left me feeling a bit naive that I could be hustled that way. But the story didn't end there. The young man, whose name was Stefan, said I could stay at his house for the two days I was stuck in London at no cost to me. I gratefully accepted his offer. Stefan was a nice guy, or so it seemed. On the second night I was there we had a couple of beers. I was a bit tipsy and ready to go to sleep. Stefan asked me if I would like another beer. I told him no. I went to the bathroom and brushed my teeth and came back to find that he had poured me another beer. These were very expensive English beers that I bought myself. I did not want them to go to waste, so I drank it despite my better judgment.

The next morning I couldn't remember anything that had happened after drinking the beer the night before. After breakfast, we walked down to a street fair. It was about a 20-minute walk. Street vendors were selling bangers and mash, which I was curious to try. There were lots of different booths and tons of interesting people, and I wound up hitting it off with a beautiful American girl. Stefan kept encouraging me to talk to her and hang out with her. Within minutes he had disappeared. I didn't even have his address, and all my belongings were at his place. The young woman told me that I should be careful—there were some Vietnamese men in that area who were known to drug men and take advantage of them while they were passed out. I tried to remember what happened the night before and I couldn't. I told her that there was a possibility that it had just happened to me.

It was getting late. I needed to find Stefan and get my stuff if I was going to make my train back to the airport on time. Back then, I had an incredible memory, so I was able to find my way from the fair back to his house. By the time I got to his place, he was upstairs, throwing my things out the window. He was yelling, saying I betrayed him and demanding to know how I could think or say that he would drug me. He must have eavesdropped on my conversation with the American girl. I started to completely lose my cool. I warned him that if he didn't stop throwing my clothes out the window, I was going to bust the door down and strangle him. I guess after seeing me put a chokehold on the agent at the airport, he thought better of it. He let me in and I got my things. I went to the airport and waited there until I took my ferry to Sweden, happy to leave London behind. My experience in London had educated me in a way I hadn't wanted or expected. But I had so much more to learn.

When I finally got to Sweden, I was exhausted. I went to sleep and had one of the strangest experiences of my life. I woke up but couldn't move my body. At the same time, I could see my body. It was as if I was up in the corner of the room watching myself lie there, awake but unable to move all night long. I wasn't sure what that was about at the time, but now I know that this is a common experience for abuse victims. A few days later I remembered something about what happened on the last night I spent in London.

I remembered waking up on the floor in Stefan's apartment, looking down, and seeing him with his mouth on my genitals. I grabbed his shoulders and flung him across the room like a basketball. It was just a tiny fragment of remembrance, just a couple of moments. Then I remembered that on the way to the street fair, Stefan had jokingly said, "You almost killed me last night." I asked him what he meant, and he just shrugged it off.

I was angry. Stefan was lucky I was in Sweden, or I'd have gone back over to his house and busted his head! I felt violated, but I was grateful it wasn't worse. I had family members who'd been raped, including two of my sisters, and while I knew my experience wasn't like anything they had been through, I now felt a whole new level of empathy for women who have been assaulted. I was grateful that I couldn't remember more. Somehow, I managed to put it out of my mind and focus on Sweden. I was in a beautiful new place and exploring my surroundings.

After a few days in Sweden, I could see the stark differences between life there and in the United States. It was mind-boggling to me. The first thing I noticed was that there was no poverty. I had only seen one homeless guy in Patrick's neighborhood. When I asked about the lack of homeless people, he told me there were no homeless people in Sweden, and that even that guy I had seen had a home; he was just a crazy old millionaire who chose his lifestyle.

I noticed there was very little crime in Sweden. Everybody I met seemed to be upper-middle class. They all drove nice cars and had nice apartments. Patrick explained their systems of education, employment, and social care for those who might need it that kept things in balance. He said that if I fell and broke my arm, I could immediately go to the doctor and get it fixed for less than twenty dollars.

Back home, I had heard socialism described as something horrific, but I found this to be the opposite. The Swedes were also much more knowledgeable about world issues. Every Swede I met knew so much more about American politics and policies than I did. At that time, Ronald Reagan was president. I knew only a few things about him. At the same time, they seemed to know everything about him: where he went to school, when he graduated, the movies he'd been in, the characters he had played, and more importantly, the policies that he supported and was working to implement, both domestically and internationally.

A week after I arrived in Gothenburg, I was invited to a formal dinner with Patrick and some of his family and friends. I was enjoying my meal, in the same way that I had been eating my entire life, when suddenly I noticed that everybody was staring at me with disgust. I looked at Patrick for guidance, and he said, "Stop eating like a stupid fucking American and look around at how to eat properly." I was pulled up short. I stopped and studied what others were doing. I became open and got past myself and asked to learn more. I had grown up with the practice of cutting up everything on the plate up at once and then gobbling up each piece. Patrick showed me that if I held my fork in my left hand and my knife in my right, I could cut only the bite I was going to eat. He also showed me that rather than shoveling my food in my mouth, I should raise the fork and knife halfway up toward my mouth, then only the fork should come all the way to my mouth as I take my bite of food. After, both hands return to the table. Not only was this a more formal and attractive way to eat, but it was also more efficient, and my food didn't go as cold. To this day, this is how I eat.

After the impromptu dining lesson, with the attention no longer on my lack of table manners, I was schooled on Ronald Reagan and his policies. They wanted to know how the American people could elect an "irresponsible clown" like Ronald Reagan as our president. They pointed out the bills and policies that Reagan was pursuing that were likely to cause long-term economic strife, particularly to the lower class, disregarding those with mental health issues, and his military spending. I had to stop them and share an embarrassing truth: I didn't pay any attention to politics. I was in college, on the track team, and I had a job. I said that I didn't trust politicians; I believed that they were all puppets for large corporations, and since I don't know who to trust, I don't vote. The Swedes were utterly appalled. They couldn't fathom the idea that someone who could vote, wouldn't.

Spending a summer in a foreign country where more than half the time I was on my own while Patrick was away at meets allowed me to grow exponentially. Sweden has beautiful rocky beaches, fresh air, beautiful weather, and gorgeous people. Yes, I had a blast. I made great friends and enjoyed beautiful lovers. I have many fond memories that I treasure. But even more than those memories, I treasure the shifts in my perception and behavior that are still with me today. Of course, there are my much-improved table manners. And I no longer wear my shoes in the house (in Sweden, like many other countries other than the United States, people do not wear their shoes in the house—it's considered unsanitary and even rude.) I take politics much more seriously, studying the issues, and voting in every election. But perhaps most importantly, I was able to see that what I am told about my country and other countries may not necessarily be true. I learned that experience (pleasant or unpleasant) is a powerful teacher. I will be forever grateful to my old friend Patrick Schulberg for giving me such a transformational summer.

That summer changed me because it made me conscious of many of my unconscious beliefs and behaviors. And it showed me how placing my attention on new beliefs and behaviors could allow me to shift them completely. I no longer had to be held back by my past, by a lack of information, by old habits, or by ignorance. Life is a great teacher for those willing to learn. And I have been fortunate to learn from other great teachers as well.

Finding Your Mission in Life

One of the most powerful experiences I have had with a teacher occurred at a Tony Robbins workshop called Date with Destiny. I was in a giant hall with four thousand other people, and he was about to guide us into an exercise to help us discover our life's mission. We jumped around, danced, high-fived, and cheered like crazy until Tony turned off the lights and had us all sit and or lie on the floor. In a meditative voice, Tony shared that he believes every single one of us has a unique mission to fulfill, that each of us has a unique voice and a unique purpose.

As his mediation was ending, I had an incredible experience. The ten-foot-tall woman made of silver light who came to me when I was four made another appearance. Like before, she shrunk herself down to my size and was floating in a full lotus position behind me. Again, she blew in my ear. Even though all I heard was the sound of someone blowing in my ear, I somehow heard her words again: "I have a very special mission for you." When the lights came on, my mission statement flowed through me and out of the pen without thought: My mission is to save the planet by spreading massive amounts of love and joy to as many people as humanly possible. As surprising as the statement was, I knew with every fiber of my being that it was true.

Having a clear mission statement gives you energetic efficiency combined with conscious directionality. Knowing your mission statement enables you to focus your energy in a clear direction. It will help you quickly and easily assess what is mission-critical and what is a distraction.

Building Your Blueprint Exercise: Creating Your Mission Statement

If you have a mission statement already, write it down. You may still want to go through this exercise to see if anything new comes up.

Find a comfortable place to lie down on a bed, couch, or yoga mat. You can also do this sitting up if meditating while sitting up is comfortable enough for you.

Start by taking deep, slow connected breaths. Remember, connected breathing means that every inhalation is connected with every exhalation with no pauses in-between. Deepen your breaths so that the inhalations last about ten seconds, and the exhalations last about ten seconds. Set a timer on your phone and do this for 7 to 10 minutes while smiling and focusing on nothing but your breath.

Next, imagine the things that you want to share with the world. Imagine the things that would make you the happiest to share with other people. Think about the gifts that you've given people in the past, personally or professionally. Take your time imagining yourself sharing your gifts with the world in a way that maximizes your potential and sense of fulfillment. Once you have a clear picture in your mind, grab a notebook and jot down as few or as many of these ideas as you can. You may have just one thought, or you may have many.

If you don't have enough inspiration to start writing your statement, use your body in a movement meditation. Turn on some music that you love and dance your heart out. While dancing, feel into your heart, and ask the question: What are my unique gifts that can be shared with my fellow humans? Or perhaps ask the question: Why am I here, who have I come here to be, and what have I got to offer the world? Then write down what comes.

By now, you should have come up with at least a few ideas that you can work into a mission statement. Remember that your mission statement is a work in progress, and it can evolve and shift over time. For now, choose a mission statement that fuels you. Write it down and take it in your heart. Once you have your mission statement written, ask yourself these follow-up questions:

- What do I need to do now to move me toward the fulfillment of my mission statement?
- What are the things that I need to learn to succeed in fulfilling my mission?
- In what ways can I fulfill this mission?

Now that you have your mission statement and have answered these questions, create a plan of action. Incorporate the answers into your daily practices. Even though I have had my mission statement for about twenty years, I still ask these questions daily. My mission statement is a bit broad, and I know that there might be many different ways in which I can fulfill it. There was a time when I believed that the venue for fulfillment of my mission had to do with teaching people about conscious sexuality and sexual mastery. Now I know that there's much more to it than that. I continue to ask: What are the different ways I can fulfill my mission and succeed in saving the planet by spreading love and joy to as many people as possible?

This question brings me new answers every now and then, even though the mission statement has not changed from that first moment at Date with Destiny, although Tony did have us all expand our statements to include caring for ourselves. My entire mission statement evolved into: *My mission is to save the planet by spreading massive amounts of love and joy to as many people as humanly possible while enjoying the process and being greatly rewarded for my efforts spiritually, energetically, physically, emotionally, and financially.*

Add this expansion to your mission statement as well. By adding these, you are ensuring that you are manifesting a kind of self-care and reward system that will allow you to be even more powerful and even more effective in creating and following through with your unique mission. It will keep you balanced and avoid the light-slave trap.

Now that you have created a clear vision, the best way to apply your new-found clarity is to learn the aligned skills you will need to bring it into reality. The next chapter looks at how you can acquire skills to support you on the journey.

"Skill is the unified force of experience, intellect, and passion in their operation."

—John Ruskin

"Repetition is the mother of skill."

—Tony Robbins

Chapter 8

ACQUIRING SKILLS

During my freshman year in high school, I met my cousin David, a black belt in Shotokan and Karate. Everyone talked about David like he was the biggest badass around, so he was a living legend by the time I met him. When we finally came face to face, I was shocked to discover he was a short guy with thick glasses who looked kind of like the clean-cut Richie Cunningham on the sitcom "Happy Days."

That day, I took David with me to the school track to meet some of my buddies. At one point, he asked if I wanted to learn some moves. He threw me around like a rag doll. Perry and Jeff, two of my closest friends throughout high school and much of my adult life, came over thinking I might be in trouble. Perry was a six-foot, 220-pound running back. Jeff was as strong as an ox. Perry told David, "I'd like to see you try that with me." David laughed and said he could take all three of us. We were skeptical. Not only did he have floppy red hair, thick glasses, and pale white skin, he was wearing skin-tight tennis shorts pulled up to his naval, socks pulled up to his knees, white tennis shoes, and a nerdy-looking striped shirt. But his looks were incredibly deceiving.

Each of us took hold of him. We had him in a head-lock, we wrapped his legs in a scissor hold, and pinned his arms behind his back. He asked if we were ready. We said yes, and in a matter of seconds, the three of us were flung out across the grass as he effortlessly broke our holds using his martial arts training. He mopped the floor with us, and it wasn't even a challenge for him. It was mind-blowing.

After that, I started training with David. Eventually, my martial arts training became more of a spiritual practice when I took up West Coast Taekwondo under Diane Murray after college. Diane earned a silver medal in the 1992 Olympic Games and a bronze medal at the 1993 World Taekwondo Championships in the bantamweight division. Her training included key philosophies on respect and responsibility, including the use of Constant and Never Ending Improvement (CANI) as our creed. We trained for five to seven hours a day, six days a week preparing to compete in tournaments. As part of our training, we meditated and spoke our goals in call-and-response fashion as they use in the military:

"Who are we?"

"West Coast Tae Kwan Do, Ma'am!"

"What's our goal?"

"CANI!"

"What does that mean?"

"Constant and Never Ending Improvement, Ma'am!"

My time studying with Diane cultivated in me great physical and mental discipline. It also taught me how to stay focused on improving myself and my skills as a life philosophy. But perhaps my most valuable lesson was how to use mindfulness and focus, as well as technique, to convert energy into power. Learning how to focus and be mindful is the cornerstone of expanding your skillset.

Mindfulness is more than just being self-aware. It's about being in tune with your spirituality and having the ability to reflect on both your positive and negative aspects. It is a specific type of awareness that harnesses the powers of energy mastery and an open mind to help you develop yourself and your skills.

Mindfulness will help you respond to any negative thoughts or emotions you may feel as you pursue acquiring new skills by saying "stop," and focusing on a positive alternative. This is a common strategy that martial artists use to silence any feelings of self-doubt and persevere, and you can apply it to everyday life. Let go of your fears and insecurities, especially those that are out of your control. There is no point dwelling on something that you cannot change, so focus on what matters most and approach your learning with a positive mindset.

Mindfulness can also help you avoid being affected by the negativity of others around you. The only thing you have the ability to change in the face of negativity is either yourself or your environment. Continue forward on the path that you chose, and don't let the distractions of others cause you to stray from that path. In martial arts, it is frequently taught to pay attention to your own actions, not those around you. Perfect your own form and don't allow thoughts of self-doubt to cause you to question your abilities or compare yourself to others.

Instead, connect your mind and your body. Keep your thoughts focused on the next step in the skill you wish to attain. Athletes focus on thoughts like, "I need to jump higher," or "I need to run faster." You, too, can stay focused on your training to achieve your goals. And remember you will get where you want to go one step at a time.

I thoroughly enjoyed my time competing and pushing myself to be undefeated in my tournament competitions. And I believe the lessons I learned from my practice still serve me today. Whether in martial arts or in life, your mind and body should be in sync for the best results, both physically and mentally. Staying mindful and present in all you do will dramatically increase your sense of happiness and success in life.

Learning Is a Journey

Learning is one of the most important things humans can do to keep their brains healthy and functioning optimally. When we take on a new task, we go through four stages of learning:

1. Unconscious Incompetence

2. Conscious Incompetence

3. Conscious Competence

4. Unconscious Competence

We start in unconscious incompetence. This means that you don't have an awareness of your incompetence quite yet. You don't know what you don't know. This stage requires a lot of humility. If we have arrogance instead of humility, we can make some big mistakes. The older we get, the more trouble we can get in because we are so used to having mastery in many areas of our lives that we can too easily believe that we know a lot about things that we actually know very little about. On the other hand, children usually know that there's a great deal about the world they don't yet understand. Even so, children, like adults, can be completely unconscious about their incompetence.

When I was four and my sister Tammy was eight, she decided we should take my father's Volkswagen bug to the candy store. She had what she thought was a great plan. She put me in the driver's seat and she crouched on the floor below me. I was supposed to do the steering, and she was going to control the brakes and gas pedal. She started the car up, hit the gas, and we crashed right through the house. "It looks so easy on TV," she said. At that moment, we moved from unconscious incompetence to conscious incompetence. We learned in a very painful and unmistakable way that we were completely incompetent at driving.

Have you had a wake-up call like this? It pulls us up short and delivers a smack-down to our ego that can sting. If you think back to some of your most embarrassing moments in life, they may have come from instances when you learned of your incompetence in a public setting. This is a place where many people stop trying and give up.

Imagine a middle school kid who happily dances in front of his mirror at home and enjoys every moment of it, not thinking about what anybody else would think. One day there is a dance at school, and when he begins dancing, everybody laughs and makes fun of him. From then on, he might just stand by the edge of the dance floor and never dance in public again. But another option is to dive deeper by taking dance lessons. In time, that same young man could end up wowing the kids at school. Sadly, when faced with our own incompetence, most of us retreat rather than push on. To stick with the driving example, if you are like most people in the United States, you had some form of driver's training as a teenager or when you first learned to drive. You were likely told your left hand must be at 10 o'clock, and your right hand must be at 2 o'clock on the steering wheel. You were told that you must check all of your mirrors, sit in a certain posture, and focus with all your attention to keep the car in the middle of your lane. You are likely still a bit nervous and burning a lot of brainpower. You move from conscious incompetence to conscious competence. In conscious competence, you can get where you want to go, but you have to really focus.

After some time has passed and you've driven enough, it becomes easier and more like second nature. You can sing along to a song you haven't heard for years, remembering the lyrics while still driving safely. At this point, you have come to the final stage in the journey, unconscious competence. Now you can drive without even thinking about it.

Owning Your Unique Voice

By remembering that success leaves clues, we can use certain philosophies, practices, and procedures that maximize success. As you think about what you want to achieve, look to others who are doing what you want to be doing, and get inspiration for your own business. Look at where and how they advertise, what kind of marketing they do, and how they frame the things that they want to share. However, it is crucial not to try to be somebody that you are not. You have to find your own voice because that is what makes you unique. You are the one thing you have that no one else will ever have.

There is a beautiful rose garden in San Jose with hundreds of rose bushes and tens of thousands of roses. Imagine yourself walking among them. The fragrant aroma of the roses stimulates your senses. As you walk, you see many different bushes filled with blossoming roses; you notice all the different shapes, sizes, and colors of these delightful flowers. Some are pink, some are white, some are orange, some are red, and some are multicolored. Some are tiny, some are large, and some are gigantic.

I have reinvented myself many times over the years. And I have managed to find success each time. I always thought of that rose garden when I was starting out on a new venture. It was how I kept myself from the trap of comparing myself to others. I had been given the gift of a poignant story about the unique beauty of roses that served me well.

Professor Keith Johnstone, author of *Improv, the improvisation Bible*, was my acting teacher for a short while. Keith tells the story of how he would go to a home for women with emotionally challenging disorders. Every Tuesday, he would meet with one specific woman, and they would walk through the rose garden. She would walk through the rose bushes and notice the differences between their colors and fragrances while celebrating the beauty and splendor of her experience. She would say, "Oh my! Look at all the beautiful flowers!" as she would smile and giggle. It was like therapy for her.

One Tuesday, Keith was unable to attend his weekly meeting with this woman. Instead, one of the nuns took his place and walked with this woman through the Rose Garden. Unfortunately, this time was different. When the woman started to express her joy and wonder about all the beautiful flowers, the nun took her to one particular flower, saying, "Come here and look at this flower. It is the most beautiful!" The idea of one flower being more beautiful than any of the others was more than the woman could take. The woman had a nervous breakdown right there in the rose garden. She went catatonic. The following week when Keith came to visit, she was still catatonic. Fortunately, Keith was able to provide a redo, a reenactment, where he brought her back out to the Rose Garden and explained that not everybody has the gift of seeing that all flowers are equally beautiful.

No matter what your unique voice is, it is perfect and beautiful and needed. There is no one else who can say what you can say or gift that you can give in the exact way that you can. My wish for you is to clearly see that in the same way that the no two flowers are exactly alike and yet all are beautiful, human beings are vastly different and your unique voice is also beautiful.

Building Your Blueprint: Your Unique Voice

Let's do some work to help you find your unique voice. Begin by getting into the peak state. You can do this by meditating with connected breathing and smiling, or by playing your favorite music while dancing and smiling.

Next, sit in a meditative position with your spine erect, your feet flat on the floor, and your palms facing up resting on your legs. Play the Essentials meditation, following it with all of your attention and a smile on your face. Next, say, "I have a unique voice. There is nobody else on earth like me." Repeat that mantra joyfully for several minutes.

Bring your hands together in prayer pose, raising them up until the backs of your thumbs touch the front of your heart chakra and chest. Then lift your hands together up past your throat past your face as high as you can. As you open your hands, imagine that you are gently grabbing a little spark of light that is floating above your head. This spark is your own unique sun's ray. Slowly lower your hands, envisioning that you are bringing your unique essence into your body. Starting with the crown of your head, feel it coming down and in as it moves between your eyebrows and your third eye, into your throat, and down into your core. Complete the process by bringing your hands to rest over your genitals.

By doing this, I want you to imagine that you have tuned in to your own unique frequency. From this place, imagine tuning more deeply than ever before into who you are and why you're here. By tuning in to your own unique essence, you should have a felt sense of how special and unique your perspective is. It is from this place that you shall share your gifts, thoughts, and experiences.

Remember that there is no one like you. No one has had the exact same experiences as you. Share your uniqueness through your words and actions. Combining the aspects of your individuality with proven steps for success, you will be able to successfully cultivate, own, and express your unique vision through your individual voice.

Creating Evolutionary Content Exercise

Now that you are owning your unique voice more and improving your capacity for self-realization, you are ready to start creating content for those you wish to serve.

Step 1: Evaluate

Locate the Creating Evolutionary Content worksheet in the Soldier of Love Workbook. (You can download your free workbook at **SoldierofLoveWorkbook.com**.) For this process, you will look at what you think the world needs that you know you can provide. Start with single words like peace, love, adventure, safety, or whatever comes to mind.

Step 2: Focus

Review your work and add to your list through the lens of your specific mission. Let's say that your mission is to help underprivileged children claim their power so that they can heal from the wounding of being abandoned by their parents. Or perhaps your mission is to work with women or the transgender community. Maybe you are focused on entrepreneurs. Whatever the focus is, write it down on the Focus line. Then, continuing down the sheet, go back through and add any additional words or phrases that your audience may need that you haven't yet captured.

Step 3: Expand

In the Expand section, write a short statement expanding on each item. Aim for a paragraph or two for each one. What are the things that you like to teach about that subject? How do you want to teach them? What formats can you use to present that material? Videos, e-books, social media posts, stories, or quizzes? Keep fleshing out each subject area with specific nuggets of wisdom that you have to offer and creative and varied ways to provide that wisdom. By the end, you will have a large number of ideas for content creation that align with your mission and serve and inspire your audience.

What's Next?

The process of creating content is never-ending, so have fun with it and record everything. No idea is a bad idea. Not at this stage anyway. As you move into actually creating the words, images, and framework for your ideas, you'll need to think about how to organize everything, so it doesn't become overwhelming or unwieldy.

Take care to preserve and protect your content ideas and the content you generate. If you are using a notebook and writing by hand, take care not to lose it and keep it safe from water and fire. If you are working on a computer, consider using a program or online service that automatically saves and stores your work. There's nothing more demoralizing than losing your work because your hard drive fails and your data isn't recoverable.

Time to Be Seen!

To be successful and make a difference with your evolutionary content, you must be willing to put yourself out there. Even the wisest and most inspiring person makes little impact until their message is shared. Your work, your point of view, and your message are valuable. Make sure that the people who need it will hear it.

One of the most direct ways to establish yourself and amplify your voice is by writing a book. It can be as little as thirty pages and even published solely as an e-book, or it can be a 300-page manuscript picked up by a major publishing house. What's important is that you gather your thoughts and collect the lessons you have learned so that they may be shared with others. You may want to write a memoir, or a guidebook, or course material. Or you may just have some life-lessons you'd like to leave for your kids.

The following is an outline that you can use to organize your writing.

Build Your Blueprint: Be Seen by Writing a Book

Before you begin, listen to the Essentials meditation to get yourself prepared and in a peak state.

You can use the worksheet in the Soldier of Love workbook for this exercise or just follow the steps below:

- Who will you write for? Think of one of your clients, students, friends, or family members that you have helped already or would like to help with your wisdom. This person will become your "Ideal Reader."

Answer these questions about your Ideal Reader:

- What is their biggest pain point?
- What is their "dream come true?"
- Why are you a reliable source of helpful information for them on this subject?

As you expand on these questions, you will be creating content for your introductory chapter or chapters.

How Will You Help Your Reader?

Think of three or more steps, qualities, or insights that you can share with your Ideal Reader to help them move from their pain point to their dream come true. These can become your chapters. Expand on each of these so that they have concrete and actionable information. List the pitfalls and challenges that you or others have faced on this journey. And complete your book with a concluding chapter that summarizes and clarifies what you want your Ideal Reader to know so that they can be changed for the better after reading your book.

How Will You Share Your Book?

Once you have your book written, it's a good idea to have someone edit it for you. You can hire someone on websites like Upwork and Fiverr if you plan to self-publish as an e-book or even as a print book. You can also find people to layout the interior of the book for you, as well as design a cover. If you would rather not handle all of this yourself, you can hire a publishing team (mine is Flower of Life Press) to improve, edit, publish, and launch your book. Or you can go the traditional route of writing book proposals to larger publishing houses. This route has all the benefits of mainstream publishing if your book is picked up, but it is usually a slower and more competitive path.

Doing More with Your Book

The book is just a beginning. It's a way to help you collect and organize your work. If you are ready to uplevel your efforts as a Soldier of Love, consider creating online programs and group mastermind programs based on your book to help spread the word. You can also use the information in your book for blogs and articles or posts on social media. One of the most effective and enjoyable ways to help spread your message is to participate in joint ventures with others in your field. Look for people who are offering online summits and ask to be part of the speaker lineup. They will interview you, and you can share the key points from your book as your message. You can also look for podcasts by people who are well-known in your field of expertise. Focus on those who interview guests on their shows. Don't be shy about putting yourself forward as a possible podcast guest. Or you may even want to make your own podcast and invite others from your field to join you on your show.

Don't expect yourself to do this all at once. It can take a year, or many years, to move through this process. Or, if you are super motivated and have the right support, it can be done in a matter of months. If all this sounds both overwhelming and exciting, you are on your way.

Now that you know what skills will help you to bring your vision into the world, the next step is following through by taking massive action. The unfortunate truth is that most people, even when feeling inspired or guided by a project, won't end up following through. One statistic says that more than 90 percent of the people who buy a book or program never finish it. Don't be like most people. The next chapter will give you some tips on how you can take action and follow-through, as well as support you in owning all of your power, which means taking responsibility for your success and failures as you seek to be a Soldier of Love.

*"Do you want to know who you are? Don't ask. Act!
Action will delineate and define you."*

—Thomas Jefferson

"Action is the foundational key to all success."

—Pablo Picasso

Chapter 9

TAKING MASSIVE ACTION

ave you ever noticed how life doesn't flow in a straight line? We plan and act and make new plans, all striving to get to our goal in the most direct and expedient route. And yet, over and over, life takes us on the scenic route instead.

During my senior year in high school, I was scouted by several universities, including the University of California-Los Angeles, University of California-Irvine, University of California-Santa Barbara, and San Diego State. I was a high jumper on the track and field team. I was undefeated all through high school, having broken the school high jump record three consecutive years. If I could jump 6 feet 10 inches in the CCS championships, I would get a full scholarship to several of these schools. I was consistently jumping between 6 feet 6 inches and 6 feet 8 inches during the regular season, and usually jumped a lot higher at the end of the season. I planned and executed my workouts so that I would be able to jump higher at the end of the season. It was two days before league finals, and I was clearing 6 feet 8 inches easily on a fairly regular basis; 6 feet 10 inches was within reach.

I continued preparing and was competing in smaller meets. At one of these smaller meets, I got stung by a bee on the ring finger of my right hand. My hand immediately swelled up to the size of a catcher's mitt. Fortunately, I was still able to jump in the meet, and I managed to take first place. Unfortunately, less than two weeks later, I stepped on a bee with my right foot and was stung again. It was just three days before the CCS championships where college recruiters were planning on watching me jump 6 feet 10 inches. My foot swelled up so big that I had to borrow a shoe from the largest guy on the track and field team. He had a size fifteen shoe. I wore a size nine usually, and I still could barely fit my foot in it. I was unable to tie it, so we taped it closed.

The day of the finals came, and I was unable to clear 6 feet 10 inches, so I did not get the scholarship offers I was hoping for. I still took first place in the meet, but my highest jump was only 6 feet 7 inches. Disappointment all around. Without the scholarship, I wasn't able to go on to college. We just didn't have the financial resources to make it happen. But rather than giving up, I decided to go to the local junior college and jumped there for a couple of years, hoping to get scouted again and increase my odds of getting a scholarship.

In junior college, my plan came together and I was recruited by San Diego State to join their track team. I was majoring in psychology and loving life. Then the unexpected happened, and my life took a dramatic turn in a new direction. My girlfriend told me she was pregnant, so we got married and prepared to welcome our child into the world. Becoming a father while I was still in college was not in my plan, but I was determined to rise to the challenge. I took on several jobs and was a full-time student and on the track and field team.

Meanwhile, it became clear that my new wife struggled with mental health and addiction. We spiraled into relationship dysfunction, separated, and then divorced. Sharing custody was rough.

Eventually, I gained full custody of my son. As a dad, I let go of many of the plans I had for myself, including my goal of being a professional sports advisor, so I could make a stable income and be the best father I could be. I worked for my father's locksmith company for a couple of months to save some money. Within six months of graduating from college, I bought my uncle's locksmith company called Lockman with a store in old town Los Gatos, California. Several years later, I purchased The Garage Door store and built that business into a thriving organization. We were happy and healthy—or so I thought.

I don't know how it happened, but I developed two hernias, which required surgery. I had just finished having my second hernia surgery and was recovering in the hospital when a friend visited me and gave me some profound advice. She told me that in the Taoist tradition, hernias are considered a sign that a man is giving away too much of his life force energy and not taking enough care of his own energetic needs, thereby causing him to burst from the inside out. She said that if I didn't make a drastic change, I would not live past the age of fifty-two. I was thirty-five.

It was spooky how real her words felt to me. They struck a chord, and for that reason, I completely believed her. She knew a little bit about my life and that I supported my son, my girlfriend, my parents, and my younger brother financially. I had employees counting on me. And I was repeatedly called upon to address the needs of those around me. After she left, I looked up in the air and asked out loud, "How am I supposed to change this shit?"

As I lay back in the hospital bed, my arm hit the remote control and the television came on. There was Tony Robbins with his gigantic energy, gigantic body, gigantic message, and pretty much gigantic everything yelling at me with his inspiring voice. "Are you looking to make change in your life?" he boomed.

Hell, yes.

I was committed to taking massive action to change my life's trajectory and stop giving away all of my life-force. I ordered and read Tony's books and signed up for his courses. Eventually, I graduated from Tony's Mastery University and joined his volunteer staff. Because I recognized and acted on the signs and signals that I was given, my life up-leveled in ways I could never have imagined.

Pushing Past Blocks to Take Action

Have you ever had the experience of talking to someone who constantly complains about their quality of life, but rarely does anything to change? I know I have, many times. It can be quite draining. I have a friend who refuses to go out and get a job because he's certain that he will win the lottery. The irony is, when I asked him when the last time he played the lottery, he couldn't even remember. He is engaged in a destructive and damaging form of magical thinking that keeps him broke and always stressed about money. And it has ruined several relationships for him.

Spiritual people can be the worst about this. Perhaps you watched "The Secret" or read Deepak Chopra's book, *The Spontaneous Fulfillment of Desire*. Or maybe you are studying the teachings of Abraham Hicks or some other teacher who is steeped in the very real power of manifestation that all humans possess. What these teachers are offering is potent and important stuff. Getting your mindset right and knowing that you can call into your life that which you desire is essential.

But it's only half of the equation.

To actually manifest something, you need to move out of the realm of ideas into the realm of action. The action is required to put the energy you generate in motion. Movies like "The Secret" inspire people to have hope. However, the real secret is using the laws of nature appropriately and effectively to get what you desire. And in the laws of nature, activity is a predominant factor in success. The bees have an abundance consciousness—they know that pollen is everywhere. But they don't sit in the hive waiting for it to come to them. They get out of the hive and use their innate ability to find the pollen they seek, and then they return home with it.

You can hope, dream, and meditate. You can read every book published and watch every show available. But if you do not get off your butt and take action, the odds are you are just going to find yourself on the same couch years later rather than achieving your goals.

Soldiers of Love know that taking massive action needs to be part of our daily habits. It is not enough to take action once in a while. It needs to be done every day. Even if some days are small actions, it's the consistency that matters. You are sending a strong signal to the Universe that you not only believe your dream is possible, but you are also acting like it is, and doing so daily. Imagine this: You want to have a clean and bright smile. You get the "download" that you should brush your teeth and floss every day. You also get the "hit" that you should avoid drinking tons of black coffee and quit smoking. But, all the wishing in the world will not remove stains off of your teeth if you do not act. You can go to a dentist every six months and they can chip off some of the plaque and sometimes even bleach your teeth, but that is not enough. It's what you do *every day* that matters most.

When I was a child, a couple of inspirational characters in the fitness world captured my attention. One was Jack Lalaine, who did jumping jacks and push-ups and sit-ups that inspired me to do the same. I also saw magazine and newspaper ads for Charles Atlas that left a strong impression on me. The ads showed a couple, a pretty woman and a smaller man, sitting at the beach. Then a bigger, more muscular man would walk up and kick sand in the smaller man's face. The smaller man was intimidated and humiliated—but inspired to take massive action. He joined the gym and showed up for his workouts every day for a couple of hours, then when the next summer came, and he went to the beach, nobody kicked sand on him anymore.

I know several men who had similar experiences. They were small and got picked on a lot, so they became motivated to take action. They went to the gym a lot, and some even hired a personal trainer. Many of them wound up being professional bodybuilders. They shifted from feeling powerless to taking this action, which, for them, transformed their life and their self-image. I have met others whose inspirational characters were musicians, actors, or poets. Following the footsteps of their heroes, many of them also became famous actors, musicians, and poets. There are many of these stories. You probably know someone in your own life who took action and made significant changes; people who went from having nothing to having everything that they desired. Maybe even you! One thing that all of these people have in common is that to make their dreams come true, they needed to take action on a daily basis.

If you are ready to take action, you may want to look into a couple of programs and people I have found helpful (or my own mastermind program, **SoldierofLoveMastermind.com**):

- Knowledge Brokers Blueprint (KBB) by Tony Robbins and Dean Graciosi: **Mastermind.com**
- Conscious Media Relations, founded by Jackie Lapin: **ConsciousMediaRelations.com**

Personal Power and Accountability

Growing up in different neighborhoods, mostly on the diverse east side of San Jose, California, I was used to being an outcast. As a blonde with blue eyes, physically, I stood like a sore thumb. However, truth be told, I fit in much more easily in the east side schools where I was a minority than I did at my predominantly white high school. I *looked* like everyone else, but I wasn't immediately well-accepted. In my first few weeks at Westmont High School, I recall walking past people and hearing them say things like, "Here comes that freak."

I worked to prove my value as an athlete to earn respect and make friends. But even then, some just found me off-putting. Maybe it was my confidence; perhaps it was my looks, the way I dressed, how I walked or talked, or maybe it was simply my energy. I don't really know. Some people in my circle loved me, but there always seemed to be others that hated me—like oil and water that just couldn't mix. Somehow, I couldn't live up to the expectations that these people had of me. I didn't know what to do to meet them—or if there was even anything I *could* do.

When I started teaching workshops, this dynamic popped up again. There were obvious expectations people had of me in that role, and then there were less obvious or invisible expectations that showed up from time to time. Eventually, I came to expect that at most workshops, I would need to be prepared to hold space for and process with one or two students. Sometimes it was women, sometimes men. It seemed they were triggered by my looks, behavior, or even just my presence. I have come to understand that, aside from the times when in my humanness I was insensitive to someone or made an occasional blunder, much of the content was coming from some disowned shadow projection. Something about me was irritating because it reminded them of another person, or some unclaimed part of themselves that they projected onto me.

If you have taught workshops or coached clients for any length of time, you may be familiar with this dynamic.

Several years back, I taught an 11-day energy workshop hosted by executive leadership firms Mobius and McKinsey. As part of my offering, people could book private sessions with me to do energy work. A man booked a session with the request that I help him step more fully into his masculine energy. At the beginning of the session, he asked me if I could hold the "bucket" for him. This term is used when somebody wants to speak their pain without any feedback.

He started by saying that none of what he would share had anything to do with me and not to take it personally. Then he went into a place of deep rage. His eyes were red, and the veins on his neck were protruding. He launched into a litany of the hatred that Jewish people had for people who look like me. "I hate you and your high cheekbones and square jawline and fucking blue eyes. You look exactly like the men who locked up and murdered my relatives and raped my ancestors! I hate the way women's panties get wet every time you walk in the room. I hate how you stand, how you walk, and that fucking smirk on your goddamn face. I hate your protein shakes and the raw cashews that you eat sitting at your chair. I hate that all the women want to work with you. I fucking hate you and everybody that looks like you! You make me sick!"

He then physically mimicked me, making a caricature out or my walk and facial expressions. The harsh and ugly comments went on for the better part of an hour. I continued holding space for this man as he siphoned out all the dark energy of his projections. I focused on staying grounded. I formed the edge of my auric field into a point, like the bow of a boat, so that the unwanted energy could split like the water of a lake and move past me. This allowed me to stay in my power and not be forced to uproot my grounding cords. It was *not* an easy task.

I felt very proud that I was able to provide this experience for this man. I was glad that he found so much value in it. But, it took a great deal of effort not to take on his comments. I admit that I did feel a little self-conscious after that while I sat in my seat, eating my raw cashews and drinking my protein shake. Every time I entered the room, I noticed him watching me and felt a little self-conscious about how I walked and stood. Even though it did not take me out of my experience as a teacher and a practitioner, it did have an impact on me in the days that followed. Even so, my overall feeling was one of gratitude that I was able to help this gentleman. At the end of the workshop, he thanked me profusely and told me that I gave him one of the biggest gifts that he had ever received. I can completely understand his pain and anguish around the horror that the Jewish people suffered in Nazi Germany and his need to defuse his anger, which had been projected on to me.

Most people are unaware of how they project their shadow material outward onto others. It's a huge cultural problem. We do it with both the dark side of the shadow and the golden shadow. When we raise people up on pedestals—teachers, celebrities, bosses, lovers, friends—we are often projecting our positive attributes on to them. They may or may not possess these attributes. Either way, eventually, they will disappoint us. They will fall from the pedestal on which we have put them. And often, as they fall, we rail at them for daring to be human.

In most cases, situations like this can be resolved by conscious conversations. It takes courage to share openly about unmet expectations and to own our part in the outcome. But it is necessary so that the appropriate amends can be made and, hopefully, the relationship can be repaired. Or at least there can be a loving parting of ways.

It seems like we have made a national pastime out of waiting for people to fail or fall short and then jumping in with great self-righteousness and "call-out" or "cancel" culture to seek to do as much damage as possible. Everyone has an opinion on how mistakes should be handled—even if they lack any details of the situation, or have only heard only a small number of cherry-picked bits of information. In those moments, we close ourselves off to the deeper, more complex truth. We fail to see or examine our own biases. We form opinions and hold fast to them, even when contradictory information is available. We all do this. So we must become aware of this tendency.

As you seek to do good and make the world a better place, you will at times disappoint people who come to you for help. You will make mistakes. You might even cause someone to hurt. I know I have. Once, just a few days after my mother had died, I fell asleep in the middle of a Tantra session. My client was understandably angry and hurt that in that vulnerable setting, I could just nod off. I apologized profusely and explained that I had not been able to sleep during the preceding weeks with my mother's illness and death. She understood and forgave me, but I realized I should have initially rescheduled that appointment. I wasn't ready to go back to work. I needed more time to grieve and heal.

Out of the thousands of sessions I have performed as a Tantric facilitator, there were a handful of times that I failed to support the client in the way they most needed because I was unable to read them or the situation properly. These were times when I was simply not at my best and didn't measure well enough to provide the experience they needed, especially when they could not articulate what they wanted.

In 2017, after more than sixteen years of service without complaint, I found myself the target of a very public "call-out" situation. Several women became part of an effort by a blogger to depict me as an abuser. I was shown letters detailing some of their concerns. One of the women felt that I talked too much about myself when she came for a session in my new home in Topanga, California. She was angry because she believed I hadn't paid enough attention to her. Another who accused me of crossing a boundary in a session with her, eventually confided in me that she only participated in the blog post because she was angry that I had ignored her at a wedding. Another was upset because a friend and colleague of ours had refused to commit to a monogamous relationship with her after they had sex. In her hurt and anger, she accused him of rape, and I was guilty by association.

Coming from the background that I did, I had a pretty thick skin. But these comments stung. These women were experienced *Tantricas* whom I cared for and considered to be friends and colleagues. I knew, and they knew, that what they were saying was far from the truth. I am not the first, nor will I be the last, to experience such a campaign. But you can't allow hollow concerns like these to derail you from your work when you know with certainty that they are not true.

On the other hand, when you know you have made mistakes or caused hurt, it is essential to listen, learn, and course-correct as thoroughly as possible. Mixed in with the fabrications in that blog was the incident that I most regret in my career. It centers around the work I was doing with a woman who had suffered sexual abuse in her past. I have worked with hundreds of women with similar backgrounds, so I was confident I could help her, too. She had also studied Tantra and was a newly practicing Dakini. In her initial interview, she said that she wanted to experience the most advanced forms of Tantric practice with me. In sessions, she aggressively pushed to make it happen, once even crossing my spoken physical boundary in a significant way. This should have been a red flag for me. I should have stopped working with her after that. But in my pride, I ignored it, thinking I could help her. She was making significant progress toward her goal. Eventually, at her continued urging, I did allow one session to include a very short experience of deeper practice. It seemed to be powerfully therapeutic, and in her post-session feedback, she shared that she felt peaceful and happy.

Later that year, she shared with our mentors and me that she felt I had violated the initial boundaries we had set. She was in great pain and confused about her feelings for me. I was heartbroken and did what I could to make amends, including at one point offering to re-fund her money. But it didn't prove to be enough. Several months later, she accused me of rape and filed a small-claims case against me, which she eventually lost. Her story was included with the others in the same blog. To this day, I wish for her sake and mine that I had made a different choice, that I had held my boundary.

Even though I knew much of the "call out" in that blog was a mis-characterization of the events that transpired, I also knew I was fully and completely responsible for everything that happens in my life and in my sessions. To do what I could to make amends and create space for healing, I made a heartfelt apology to the individuals involved and to our Tantra community. I changed how I did my practice. I went into a time of deep personal reflection. And, I eventually decided to semi-retire. I continued the hard work of forgiving myself for ignoring the red flags, making the wrong call, and letting others and myself down. And then, I resolved to live my life and continue my work in the world without anger or bitterness in my heart. Unforgiveness is a poison that never ends. There is too much work to do in the world, and staying stuck in the past just keeps that work from being done.

In today's internet age, where accusations, rumors, and gossip can fly around your community in seconds, social media take-downs are more common than ever. If you have the unfortunate experi-ence of being on the receiving end of this kind of action, take heart in knowing where you stand. If you have a mess to address, do so as straightforwardly as you can while not giving your power away to anyone else. Clean it up from a place of love and compassion for all involved. And then give yourself and others the permission to move on.

Notice the Habit of Inaction

When things get hard, it's tempting to think about giving up, giving up on yourself, giving up on each other, giving up on the world. But this is something a Soldier of Love cannot allow. The harder things get, the more we are needed. If you find yourself sinking into inaction, you must resolve to intervene. The first and most important intervention is offering yourself compassion. There's no need to rake yourself over the coals for having a down moment, or a down day—or three. Compassion doesn't insist that you become falsely cheery or pretend that you aren't struggling. It gives you space to feel what's real for you, but it also loves you through it. Compassion is the love that leads you home to yourself. It helps you own your sadness, hurt, shame, or self-doubt, but it won't allow you to pitch your tent there.

Inaction is a sink-hole. Compassion is the first act that will allow you to move on to the next action. When you are feeling stuck in the place of inaction, doing your energy mastery techniques is a simple solution. Using the Essentials meditation will help you ground, shield, and energize yourself in just a few minutes. Think about your Reichian pattern. What is it that comforts you? Maybe you make yourself your favorite comfort food, and you put on your favorite song and dance. Perhaps you sit outside in the sun or walk on the beach. Maybe you shower and shave and put on clean clothes. Perhaps you straighten the house or call a friend. One step at a time, you move forward.

Action of any kind will be your best friend. And if it's aligned with your mission, all the better. What will help you move the needle forward in your effort to evolve yourself and evolve the world? Find a small action, one that seems almost too small to matter, and take that action. Then celebrate, and build on it. Success is nothing but a series of small actions strung together. The discipline of doing your daily energy and spiritual practices is the best insurance against the sink-hole of inaction. Because you are committed to acting through your daily practice, you will be able to keep the energy flowing in your life.

Don't confuse rest with inaction. We all need rest, especially when we have experienced a setback or a loss. Making the conscious choice to rest, to nap, to take a day off, or to relax your attention is in and of itself an action. Being present with yourself is essential. Self-care is essential. Balance is essential. And so is your commitment to yourself and your mission. Having a vision for yourself, your life, and how you will make the world a better place will keep you focused.

Building Your Blueprint: Knowing Your Vision

This next exercise is a short but important one: Defining your vision. Your vision is an extension of your mission. The goal is to create a sense of what your life and the world look like when you have accomplished your mission and when you have worked yourself out of a job. Grab your journal or the Soldier of Love workbook and find a comfortable place to sit. Close your eyes for a few moments and connect your mind with your body. Then tune into your unique sun's ray and your unique frequency. Feel it alive in your body and allow it to glow and grow until you feel that every cell in your body is vibrating at that frequency. You know you are here for a purpose. You are on a mission. Recall that mission. Let it light you up even more. As you feel the light beginning to overflow out of your body, see it filling up your entire auric field until the egg-shaped field all around you is glowing.

Now imagine fast-forwarding well into the future. You and your colleagues, guides, protectors, and angels have been wildly successful in achieving your mission. Feel the pride and happiness dancing through your body as you celebrate a job well done. Allow yourself to look out into the world to survey your handiwork. How is the world different? How is the world better? How are the people healed, including you, your loved ones, and even those you once saw as your enemies? Notice how the dreams you have had are all manifesting. Allow yourself to feel gratitude and appreciation for yourself and the world. Let all the details sink in. How does the environment look? How are people behaving? What is the social sphere like? What are the colors, sounds, and textures of life? See it all in its completely healed and perfect state. So much so, that there's simply nothing left for you to do other than enjoy it.

After spending 5 to 10 minutes taking in all these details and enjoying the energy of this future place, pick up your pen and journal and start writing everything you see and feel. No detail is too small or insignificant to record. Take your time recording it all. Keep this vision of the future in a special place but also one that is handy. Come back to it often, dropping into the space within to really feel the emotion of completing your mission. This practice will support you in continuing to soldier on in love no matter what you see happening around you. It will help pull you toward the future that you want to create and help you leave behind that which is no longer working.

Building Your Blueprint Exercise: Making an Action Plan

Now that you have your vision, it's time to create a plan for bringing it about. This plan can include high-level tasks, like developing a year-long mastermind program, or it could have smaller tasks, like setting up an account with an email service like Mailchimp or Constant Contact. On a fresh sheet of paper, allow your ideas to spill out on the page. Don't edit the list until you have completed it. You may want to do this directly after writing your mission, or you may want to wait a day or two. Either way is fine. This is not something that you are going to do once and then never look at it again. You will be updating and refining this list all the time. So, what types of actions will you take to share your love and wisdom with the world? Here are some items that might help you get the list going. The Soldier of Love Workbook has many more ideas to help you get started (**soldieroofloveworkbook.com**).

- Build or upgrade your website
- Make a list of potential clients
- Create an irresistible free gift
- Write a book or e-book or record an audiobook
- Deepen your training with one of your teachers
- Find a new teacher to study with
- Lead masterminds, online workshops, and/or summits
- Create live events
- Develop certification courses
- Offer private coaching
- Offer private healing sessions
- Launch an affiliate programs
- Create a powerful product

"Obstacles are those frightful things you see when you take your eyes off your goal."

—Henry Ford

"The greater the obstacle, the more glory in overcoming it."

—Molière

Chapter 10

CLEARING OBSTACLES WITH MASTERFUL PRECISION

B ecoming a Soldier of Love is a never-ending process. When we reach one new layer of expression, it sets the stage for the next. We can and will enjoy each stage, each growth spurt, if we also allow ourselves to celebrate where we are. Starting is easy for some people and hard for others. And once you get started, staying engaged may prove to be a challenge. Or perhaps it will be finishing that is the hardest part. Regardless of when it happens, facing resistance is inevitable, so make a plan now to address obstacles. The question is not whether you will face obstacles; it's when and how to prepare. Facing obstacles as we grow and evolve is not to be wished away. Initiations are, after all, a vital part of the journey. They make us stronger and better.

To reframe obstacles, I like using the term "hurdles." While obstacles are designed to impede, hurdles are designed to be jumped. When I was on the track and field team in high school and college, I was very impressed at how people who ran the high hurdles could run at full speed and bound over the hurdles in front of them with seeming ease. Of course, I knew they practiced for hours to become proficient. It's a thing of beauty to watch a skilled racer as they jump, staying low to the ground, just skimming the top of the hurdles with their follow leg. The person who hit the most hurdles usually lost, while the one who was able to clear the hurdles effortlessly usually finished first, assuming they had the foot speed. As Soldiers of Love, we will face our hurdles head-on and seek to move past each one as efficiently as possible.

The following are some of the most common hurdles my clients and students have faced and some thoughts on moving past them.

Hurdle: I don't know enough yet.

There is nothing wrong with studying with a teacher or mentor. I have always trusted in the axiom that my path to success would be supported if I hired the most expensive and experienced teachers I could afford. But we must beware of the temptation to believe that one more certificate, one more class, one more workshop will finally give us that elusive sense of enoughness to cast self-doubt out of our minds. You will never know all there is to know. But you already know a lot. Whatever arena is your expertise, whether it's repairing cars, parenting with intention, or coaching couples, you have something to offer. Your life experience, training, and skills will always be better developed than others who haven't had the experience you have had. What you have to offer will have value. When you teach something for the first time, offer it as a pilot, and at a reduced price. Let people know they will be part of the process in helping you refine the course.

Hurdle: I just have to get my energy right, and then everything will fall into place.

There's a commonly shared notion that "Good things come to those who wait," or "If you build it they will come." The truth is that it takes effort to accomplish most things. This kind of thinking often comes from a desire to avoid making mistakes. So we think if we are doing it right—if we are spiritual enough—we won't have to work hard. Hard work, focus, concentration, energy, and effort are somehow viewed as proof that we aren't spiritual enough. This is complete crap. If we are *doing, doing, doing,* that is a problem. But as a Soldier of Love, you now know how to live and work in balance. Plus, you have cleared your perceptions so your mission is truly one from the heart, something that you are passionate about. So your actions should be aligned and energizing. If you don't have the energy to act, you may need to revisit the work you are doing. Just like the bees who go out to get the pollen, you will have to act to have the success you desire and deserve. And the world is counting on you.

Hurdle: I don't want to fail.

Many attempts and failures often precede success. Michael Jordan, a world-class basketball player with six NBA championships to his name, famously said, "I've missed more than 9,000 shots in my career. I've lost almost 300 games. Twenty-six times, I've been trusted to take the game-winning shot and missed. I've failed over and over and over again in my life. And that is why I succeed. Failure makes me work even harder. I've never been afraid to fail. I know fear is an obstacle for some people, but it is an illusion to me. Failure always made me try harder next time."

Our failures can be stepping stones or they can be excuses for procrastination, apathy, or blatant disregard. When it comes to preparing for life, we must embrace the truth that humans are behaviorally fallible and make many mistakes. If you cannot accept this truth about yourself and others, you will be constantly wounded and feel victimized by life. Using the law of least effort means not making the same mistakes over and over again while expecting a different response. That is the definition of insanity! As long as we learn from our mistakes, every mistake has the potential to become a gift—some of which will be life-changing for you.

Hurdle: I can't seem to catch a break.

Many people are programmed to believe that they are not enough; therefore, they will never succeed. This belief keeps them from even trying, and could be disguised as reasoning or logic by pointing out the risks or chances of failure, therefore justifying the decision not to act. The question is not what to do if problems should arise. The question is how quickly and effectively we can handle the challenges when they arise because, believe me, they will arise. It's critical that you do not allow setbacks to define you. They are just scenery on the path toward greater competence and even mastery.

Hurdle: I don't have the resources I need.

To have a healthy relationship with money, we have to take an honest look at what we believe about money. Do you see it as a necessary evil or a path to doing more good? Do you believe it's okay to have excess if others don't, or do you see that as disloyal or greedy? Do you treat the money you do have with respect and honor? Or do you avoid thinking about it or taking care of it? To develop wealth in your life, you must develop a wealthy mindset to alleviate unnecessary stress and energetic blocks to abundance.

Ultimately, wealth is doing something you love. It's better to put your focus on pursuing something you love and do it so well that people are willing to pay you for it. Let making money be the outcome, not the goal. And don't compare your success to another's success. You may need and want different things. Maybe you desire more free time or a house surrounded by nature, while someone else wants invitations to high-level events in their industry and an apartment in town. Joel Wyrick's powerful book *Developing A Wealthy Mindset* has many great suggestions for defining and building wealth. As Joel says, "When it comes to money and wealth, *like* attracts *like*."

Hurdle: I don't have enough support.

Are you frustrated because the people you add to your team are not meeting your expectations? It's important to keep looking for the right team members rather than putting up with those who aren't a good fit. Maybe you just wish you had the resources to get a bit of project-based help from a virtual assistant. Sometimes you have to get creative. Perhaps you can find a way to trade your service for some administrative support. In the short run, expanding your business team means making less money. But in the long run, it positions you for growth so that you can increase your income. Perhaps you feel stymied because you are in an unsupportive relationship. This can be rough. Try your best to schedule time for yourself and your work. Claim your space. And if your partner is open to listening, make your case for why you feel passionate about your work. If your partner expects you to choose between your soul's mission and the relationship, they may not be the best partner.

A Final Note: Don't Give Up

Make a plan now for how to clear the hurdles you will face as a Soldier of Love. If you never think about it or train for it, when you come up to a hurdle, you will freeze, or you will try and fail. It's possible that if you are lucky, you could power yourself through it. But the likelihood of getting all the way to the finish line in one piece is small if jumping every hurdle is a herculean effort. Successful entrepreneurs have tried and failed so often that they don't even flinch anymore when it comes to hurdles. That is the difference between you and them; they have tried and failed more times than you. And as a result, they have learned how to jump all kinds of hurdles. They are no longer afraid of hurdles. You can learn from their efforts to become masterful and clear your own hurdles and those put in your way so you will reach the finish line with greater success.

"Build your life on your dreams; because dreams never have bad endings."

—M.F. Moonzaje

"Our story may have any number of endings, but its start is a singular choice we make today."

—Faisal Khosa

Chapter 11

PUTTING IT ALL TOGETHER

We are at a decision point as a nation and a world. It is in these moments of decision that destiny is shaped. The evolutionary movement is inspiring people to unite and be in harmony rather than conflict. This movement is crucial to the survival of our species. I picture my two-year-old granddaughter Malia and the hopes I have for her life. I see her in her full potential, not yet burdened by the conditioning we are working to undo and move past. Can you picture a young child, perhaps a younger version of yourself, who has yet to question his or her value, who loves unconditionally and does not wonder whether they are lovable? I hope you have come a long way back toward that younger version of yourself, only now you have the added benefit of the skills, tools, and practices that will make you a powerful force for good.

This book was written for people who want to heal themselves from their past and thrive in life. It is also for those who want to help others thrive and succeed. When you achieve your goals, impact more lives, and make the world a better place, I know you will be rewarded with abundance energetically, physically, emotionally, spiritually, professionally, and financially.

I am so grateful that you have chosen to make the journey. Along the way, you have taken a hard look at the complex issues facing today's world. You know how desperately it needs an evolutionary upgrade, and you have signed up to be part of the mission to bring it about. You have committed to developing yourself so that you will have the greatest chance of success in this critical mission. You have done the exercises and activities to update and upgrade your Evolutionary Blueprint.

You have gained specific awareness and skill sets that can help you cultivate presence in your life. You have learned about energy and the tools and practices it will take to achieve mastery. You are no longer held hostage by your unconscious habits of attention and now have an awareness of your Reichian pattern structures. You have learned about living in balance and developing discipline. You are aware of the old programming that was given to you without your permission or knowledge. You have begun the work to break free from these old programs and create new, updated programs that will better support your success in the world. You know what your mission and vision are, and you are acquiring critical skills and taking aligned action to create amazing things.

Now it's time for the rubber to meet the road.

I invite you to take the Soldier of Love Pledge, to make an absolute commitment to being a Soldier of Love in your own life and in the world!

SOLDIER OF LOVE PLEDGE

I pledge my commitment to myself and my country. To honor all life and to bring about a better world.

I commit to Constant and Never-ending Improvement (CANI); to feeding my body and mind daily.

I pledge to make better choices by asking better questions, because the quality of every interaction and experience in my life is a direct reflection of the quality of questions that I ask.

I commit to being a master of my energy and doing the practices that will keep me centered, grounded, protected, and energized.

I commit to living in balance and developing the discipline to be the absolute best version of myself by nurturing my body through devotional self-care and a full personal life.

I pledge to communicate consciously and to do the loving thing whenever possible. When in doubt, I pause and ask myself what would be the loving thing to do, and do that.

I commit to using my skills to serve humanity by raising general awareness in the collective consciousness to treat everything and everyone with respect, and to help clean up and care for the Earth.

I pledge to leave everything and everyone better than I found them, and always have my presence add value.

I salute you, Soldier of Love! From this point forward, may you devote yourself to living in balance, developing discipline, and creating clarity. May you always remember that in acquiring skills and taking action, you will need to jump the hurdles that life places in front of you. Only now, you will no longer wish them away, but view them as exercises to bring out your fullest potential. Like an American Ninja Warrior who goes through an entire obstacle course, each hurdle or obstacle you overcome will make you stronger. As you tend to your daily practices, you will be able to do that with tremendous grace. You will grow in your commitment to never giving up on yourself, others, or the world.

The more of this work you master, the more masterful you will be in the world. As a Soldier of Love, you will help lead a movement that brings together the inner and outer journey toward wholeness, where we have put our swords in service to our hearts. We can leave behind the wars and violence we have created out of fear and embrace a life built on peace and love. The time is now to look around and gather to you those with a similar mission. As Soldiers of Love, we know that we won't be perfect in our endeavor, but we can and will be better. And we will be at our very best when we are all in it together. May you soldier on in Love.

Afterword

It Takes a Village

Now that you have completed your Evolutionary Blueprint, it's important to remember this isn't a "one-and-done" kind of a thing. Our programming is always in need of upgrades. By continuously upgrading, you will keep building and expanding your body's capacity to choose love over fear with greater ease and grace. You are not alone in this. You are now part of a beautiful and powerful community of like-minded individuals who support each other, hold each other in a positive light, and encourage each other always to do our very best. Become part of the active conversation. Welcome, soldier. You are loved and appreciated.

Visit **SoldierofLoveBook.com** to learn more about how you can become part of the movement.

Share your review of *Soldier of Love* by scanning the code below:

Tj Bartel, author, speaker, teacher, coach

ABOUT THE AUTHOR

With nearly twenty years of experience and proven excellence in the personal development field, Tj Bartel has mastered the skills required to succeed as a coach, author, and educator. Tj is a highly successful entrepreneur who shares his expertise in workshops, masterminds, and coaching programs worldwide. Mr. Bartel specializes in personal transformation, evolutionary education, and conscious sexuality. His techniques integrate perennial wisdom from the Taoist, Vedic, and Tantric traditions, Egyptian mystery school teachings, modern neuroscience, guided meditation, and innovative personal growth techniques. Tj's primary goal is to create lasting and meaningful change and transformation in individuals and the world. He also enjoys supporting people in creating exquisite relationships, which will ultimately lead to positive benefits for themselves and everyone in their lives.

Tj Bartel has made it his mission to bring more love to this planet and to support others who wish to do the same. He developed a keen interest in human behavior and personal growth in his teen years, which inspired him to earn a Bachelor's degree in Psychology. After attending the Tony Robbins Mastery University, Tj discovered his talents for transforming lives positively. He was so motivated that he continued to research how he could better help others across the globe in their relationships and sexual intimacy. Throughout his career, Tj has earned many advanced certifications, taking a wide variety of classes to support his mission and improve his life.

Today, Tj shares his expertise both online and through in-person workshops, having mostly retired from hands-on sexual awakening. His primary focus is on teaching, training, and writing for his Blueprints for Life series, helping a broader audience find the answers they need to be the best versions of themselves and create a more loving and conscious world.

ADDITIONAL BOOKS BY FLOWER OF LIFE PRESS

The New Feminine Evolutionary: Embody Presence—Become the Change

Pioneering the Path to Prosperity: Discover the Power of True Wealth
and Abundance

Sacred Body Wisdom: Igniting the Flame of Our Divine Humanity

Set Sail: Shine Your Radiance, Activate Your Ascension, Ignite Your Income,
Live Your Legacy

Practice: Wisdom from the Downward Dog

Sisterhood of the Mindful Goddess: How to Remove Obstacles, Activate Your Gifts,
and Become Your Own Superhero

Path of the Priestess: Discover Your Divine Purpose

Sacred Call of the Ancient Priestess: Birthing a New Feminine Archetype

Rise Above: Free Your Mind One Brushstroke at a Time

Menopause Mavens: Master the Mystery of Menopause

The Power of Essential Oils: Create Positive Transformation in
Your Well-Being, Business, and Life

Self-Made Wellionaire: Get Off Your Ass(et), Reclaim Your Health,
and Feel Like a Million Bucks

Emerge: 7 Steps to Transformation (No matter what life throws at you!)

Oms From the Mat: Breathe, Move, and Awaken to the Power of Yoga

Oms From the Heart: Open Your Heart to the Power of Yoga

The Four Tenets of Love: Open, Activate, and Inspire Your Life's Path

The Fire-Driven Life: Ignite the Fire of Self-Worth, Health, and Happiness
with a Plant-Based Diet

Becoming Enough: A Heroine's Journey to the Already Perfect Self

The Caregiving Journey: Information. Guidance. Inspiration.

Plant-based Vegan & Gluten-free Cooking with Essential Oils

Ancient-Future Unity: Reclaim your Roots, Liberate Your Lineage, Live a Legacy of Love